ANUBIS ~ an INNER G

ANUBIS ~ an INNER GUIDE

# ANUBIS

## an
## INNER GUIDE

### Judith Page

Edited by

Paul F. Newman

## ANUBIS ~ an INNER GUIDE

Copyright © 2022 Judith Page

All rights reserved, including the right to reproduce this book, or portions thereof, in any form.

The copyright for individual contributions – artwork, text, and photographs – remains with the contributors/owners.

Cover design and Layout by Judith Page
http://www.judith-page.com

drawings and photography by Alain Leroy

Font: Book Antiqua 11 point

This book is sold subject to the condition that it shall not, by way of trade or otherwise, be lent, resold, hired out, or otherwise circulated without the publisher's prior consent in any form of binding or cover other than that in which it is published and without a similar condition being imposed on the subsequent purchaser.

A catalogue record for this book is available from the British Library and the US Library of Congress
All rights reserved.

**ISBN:** 9798835271337

Hail Anpu!
May he heal your soul.
His black flame is your consciousness.
May you continue to grow and teach us.
The Gods wait for us to join them.
*Linda Kelley*

# DEDICATION

To my teachers, Dolores Ashcroft Nowicki, Don Webb,
the late Dr. Michael A. Aquino,
and Elizabeth St. George.

**Judith Page** was born in Australia. She graduated from Chelsea School of Art in London. She is a respected painter specializing in representations of Egyptian Pantheon groups with a strong emphasis on astronomy. Her work has featured on the covers of numerous magazines and books. She is a great storyteller and poet and brings mystery and magic alive.
© *Joe Page*

**Books in collaboration with other authors**
Realm of Angels (Aaron Leitch)
Guardians of the Stellar Grael (Paul F. Newman)
The Fresco of Dommoc Hall (Paul F. Newman)
Secret SHROUD (Paul F. Newman)
The Coven of Otley Drive (Paul F. Newman)
The Path of Verity Moss (Paul F. Newman)
The Lost Queen (Paul F. Newman)
The SIGIL (Paul F. Newman)
Dark Tales I (Paul F. Newman)
Daughters of Salem (Paul F. Newman)
Lords & Ladies (Paul F. Newman)
GRAEL Magazine Autumn (Paul F. Newman)
GRAEL Magazine Winter (Paul F. Newman)
GRAEL Magazine Spring (Paul F. Newman)
Costa de Mar (Paul F. Newman & Alain Leroy)
Verity Moss ~ a perpetual diary (Paul F. Newman)
Dark Tales II (Paul F. Newman)
Priestess of Anubis (Paul F. Newman)
SET The Outsider (Don Webb)
Song of SET
Song of Bast
Song of Meri-Khem
Song of the Ibaru

# CONTENTS

Acknowledgments...ix
Illustrations...x
Foreword... xii
Introduction... xiii

**Part I**
Origins ~ Judith Page... 1
Animism, Totemism and Fetishism to God
~ Judith Page... 11
How Anubis was usurped ~ Judith Page... 19
Opening of the Mouth Ceremony ~ Judith Page... 24
What is the Book of the Dead ~ Judith Page...32
Death Rituals ~ Judith Page... 38
Temples and Priesthoods ~ Judith Page... 43
Dying Twice - Osiris ~ Judith Page... 52
Rebirth and Initiation ~ Judith Page... 57
What is Heka – Magic ~ Judith Page...72
The Anubieion ~ A Dark Time ~ Judith Page...76
Canopic Jars ~ Judith Page...83
Dark Journey of the Soul ~ Judith Page...88
From Anubis to Saint Christopher ~ Judith Page... 98
Man's Best Friend ~ Judith Page ... 105

**Part II**
Saint Roch and his Dog ~ Judith Page...116
Foremost of the Westerners ~ Bill Duvendack... 121
Black Dogs in Folklore ~ Bob Trubshaw...130
Anubis: A story of ancient Egypt ~ Michael Starsheen...139
Being a visionary – Ritual of Descent ~ Dr. Tim Broussard...143

**Part III**
What is Pathworking ~ Judith Page...154
Path to Anubis ~ Judith Page and Jan Malique...158
Meaning of Invoking ~ Judith Page...166
Invoking Anubis ~ Judith Page...178
Epilogue ~ Don Webb...187
Bibliography for Part I & III...190
To write to the authors...193

## AKNOWLEDGEMENTS

I wish to thank my friend and editor, Paul F. Newman,
Don Webb, Bill Duvendack, Bob Trubshaw, Michael Starsheen,
and Dr. Tim Broussard for their wonderful contributions.
Further thanks to Alain Leroy for his superb artwork.
All assert copyright to this material in their names.

# ILLUSTRATIONS

**NOTE:** All black and white drawings by Judith Page and Alain Leroy are from photographs.
1. Sety 1st with. Khenti-Amentiu, Temple in Abydos
2. Anubis weighing the heart, Papyrus of Ani
3. Anput (Input) wife of Anubis
4. Mask of Anubis circa 1,800 – 1,200 BCE.
5. Wepwawet with *shedshed'* or, *'bundle of life'*
6. Hermanubis
7. Sobdet, tomb of Seti 1st
8. *jmy-wt* fetish
9. *jmy-wt* fetish in the tomb of Tutankhamun
10. Osiris: Tomb of Nefertiti
11. Mer-wer bull, Hatshepsut's mortuary temple
12. Anubis, Papyrus of Nu and the Papyrus of Nebseni
13. Khenti-Amentiu name on the necropolis cylinder seals for the 1st Dynasty Pharaohs
14. Earliest location of Nekhen
15. Earliest design of a temple
16. Libation pot
17. Umm el Qa'ab, 'Mother of Pots' – Abydos
18. Shu supporting the goddess Nut
19. Anubis holding the Adze, Tomb of Nefertiti
20. Wooden Adze
21. Mourners Tomb of Khonsu, Gourna
22. Mysterious Tekenu
23. Opening of the Mouth Ceremony 1 – 14, E. A Wallis Budge
24. Spell on the back of the Heart scarab
25. Heart Scarab
26. Heart Scarab
27. Weighing of the Heart: Papyrus of Ani
28. Anubis over the body of the deceased
29. Statue of mourning Isis, Louvre, Paris
30. A scene of mourning women at an Egyptian funeral
31. Embalming priest with a jackal mask
32. Wepet, Renpet New Year Festival, Luxor Temple
33. Thoth judging of the dead by the God Osiris

34. Isis guides the Boat of the Night through the Duat
35. Plan of Karnak Temple
36. Vestibule, Opet Temple
37. Map of the Saqqara necropolis by Jacques de Morgan
38. Tombes des chiens, Jacques de Morgan
39. Four Canopic Jars
40. Drawing of Akh, Ba, Ka & Khat after Isha Schwaller de Lubicz
41. Khnum fashioning a human on his potter's wheel, Luxor Temple
42. Ammit, The Devourer, Papyrus of Ani
43. 2nd century Roman funeral shroud
44. 17th century icon of St. Stephen and St. Christopher
45. Egyptian god Anubis, with halo disc, Cairo Museum
46. St. Christopher represented as a giant of a man
47. Greek icon, St Christopher, Patron Saint of travellers
48. Vintage St. Christopher medallion
49. Two Dogs Palette, Naqada II period (3500-3000 BCE)
50. 11th Dynasty tomb stela depicting Horus Wah-ankh Intef II
51. Sloughi and Saluki, Tomb of Mereuka
52. Drawing of hunting dogs
53. Young boy with a pet can, ostraca
54. Princess Elizabeth and King George VI with their corgis
55. St. Roch, Church in Skakavac, Croatia
56. St. Roch with an angel
57. Rev. P. L. Thevis
58. Gates of St. Roch Cemetery, New Orleans
59. Hermanubis
60. Xolotl
61. Mictlantecuhtli
62. The Hound of the Baskervilles
63. Medieval woodcut of 'Shuk'
64. Black Dog of Somerset
65. Gabriel Hounds or Gabble Retchets
66. The Bungay Black Dog depicted in the town's weathervane
67. Prince Rupert and his 'devil dog'
68. Bas relief, Hapi, Temple of Philae, Aswan
69. Corn growing from Osiris's body, bas relief, Karnak Temple
70. Paulina in the Temple of Isis by Fortunino Matania

# FOREWORD

## by Don Webb

Anubis is almost the logo for esoteric Egypt. You've seen him in colophons. You've seen him in movies. You can buy little idols of him in little shops of occult bric-a-brac. The Egyptians took two sorts of canines – man's best friend and the now extinct Egyptian red wolf and made two guardian gods, Wepwawet (the wolf) and Anubis (the dog). He could lead the Pharaoh's army, the boat of Re, and the souls of the dead. He was the Egyptian prototype of the shaman, the professional crosser of realities. He is the black dog that any folklorist encounters – if you research your own city you'll find "black dog" sightings. In that rather odd sense, he is the most visible of all the Egyptian pantheon.

Colonial scholars wanted to deemphasize him and tried saying he was a jackal. Even the Egyptians themselves tried to cage the dog by incorporating him into the Osirian mythos by the middle dynasties, but they kept the shaman's mask for the Opening of the Mouth ceremonies. The Greeks missed the boat by identifying Hermes with Thoth. Thoth isn't dangerous enough, funny enough. The great Egyptian Hermes was and is Anubis.

He was the only one of the old gods that never went away. Whether as the ghost of Wild Edric or the prototype of St. Christopher. Anubis couldn't be banished. As a dog, he is faithful. He is willing to help you enter other realms safely just as he has for five thousand years. As a wolf, he is fierce, wild, and willy – and willing to transform you into one of his packs. He has chosen to live alongside mankind 30.000 years ago and he is making a return at this stressful time. As he always has.

Judith Page is a rational scholarly human. Judith Page was also chosen to help some of the old gods back into their seats. We see them all around us – in Marvel movies, in modern art – let's renew old partnerships with careful objective scholarship and wild magical ecstasy. It's time to throw an old god a bone!

# INTRODUCTION

## by Judith Page

Originally when I began writing this book, the intention was to just concentrate on the ancient Egyptian god Anpu, commonly known as Anubis. However, this canine being is not only confined to this ancient land but enjoys a far broader spectrum. He has been popular in media culture longer than any other Egyptian deities and has more often been falsely portrayed as a sinister god of the dead. Since the early twentieth and twenty-first centuries, he gained recognition through books, video games, and films, where artists would give him, an evil presence accompanied by an equally dangerous army. Two films that spring to mind are *Stargate* (1997) and *The Mummy* (1999), the latter a remake of the original from 1932. No doubt, you can recount more. Yet despite his degenerate reputation, his image is still the most recognisable of the Egyptian gods, and replicas of his statues and paintings remain popular. There's much more to Anubis the dog.

With origins dating back to the palæolithic period, dogs have had an unusually close association with humans, sharing their hearths and defending the home at night while working during the day as shepherds or hunters, as well as sharing their food and water. This intimate symbiotic link between dogs and humans is represented in early literature, where canines appear to have strong ties to the Otherworld. However, this is not exclusive to hounds, since numerous animals, ranging from bulls and boars to owls and cuckoos, have strong links with deities, leading to ceremonial adoration of these creatures. Archaeological data and legend provide several examples of dogs playing a very specialised function in human society. They are the 'psychopomps', the guides on the paths to the Otherworld, the guardians of the 'liminal' zone at the boundaries of the worlds.

A clear example from British archaeology is two dogs found at the Flag Fen Neolithic/Bronze Age complex near Peterborough. This site was undoubtedly a major focus for funereal rituals over many centuries. These animals appear to have been ritually killed to serve as spirit guardians. At Caldicot in Gwent, another Bronze Age site provides evidence for a dog buried in a manner that strongly suggests a role as ritual guardian. Few people were buried during the Bronze Age. If funeral fires were set up by major rivers, as Hindus do in India today, we can only guess how the dead were buried. Did they leave this world like the 'Towers of Silence' of the Parsis in India, a group of people who lived before all the major world religions? During the Bronze Age, people might have seen dogs and other animals gnaw on human bodies and break them down into small pieces. Such a grisly sight would reinforce the dog as the species most suited to act as a psychopomp.

Pre-technological cultures also thought that the 'essence' of food is absorbed by people who eat it. This is true even though many don't believe it. The idea is that the body and soul are both taken in by a dog when it eats the corpse. It's interesting to note, that pigs and boars are also big eaters of carrion, which could be why Freya's favourite animal is the boar, which is also linked to the dead from a battle. It might also be why the 'Tombs of the Eagles' in Orkney are so-called because the human bones were found next to the bones of large raptors. If the rich were buried in a chamber tomb, and sea eagles carried the bodies and souls of the dead to the sky, it would be normal to think that this was what happened.

In North African countries the dog is less prevalent as a scavenger than is the jackal. 'The dead man is at one and the same time in heaven, in the god's boat, under the earth, tilling the Elysian fields, and in his tomb enjoying his victuals.'

His name 'Anpu' is from the same root as the word for a royal child, 'inpu'. However, it is also closely related to the word 'inp' which means 'to decay', and one version of his name Inp or Anp more closely resembles that word. As a result, it is possible that his name slightly changed once he was adopted as the son of the King, Osiris. He was known as 'Imy-ut'; 'He Who is In the Place of Embalming', 'nub-ta-djser'; 'lord of the sacred land'. This may give us a clue as to why he was so closely associated with death. But who was Anubis, and how did he rise from being man's best friend to fetish and a major deity?

Whoever he was, he was an extremely ancient god pre-dating Osiris. His name appears in the oldest mastabas of the Old Kingdom and the Pyramid Texts and as well as being a guardian and protector of the dead, Anubis became associated specifically with the embalming process and funeral rites.

The magnificence of the temples, the belief system or the Mysteries as they were more generally referred to, are well named. From their very beginnings to the present day they continue to be mysterious, cloaked in an atmosphere of profound secrecy. The Anubis figure may have been intended to combine the role of a guard and a custodian of secret things. 'He who is over the secrets.' It is this secrecy we aim to tap into.

As we move forward towards Christianity, often the suggestion is seen in historic accounts that Saint Christopher was the product of a tryst between a human being and an Anubis, a demon-like creature based on the Greek Anoubis, which came from the Egyptian's jackal-headed god who led the dead to judgment. We will explore this notion in the book.

The scholarly has been balanced with the magical element of this deity. The Jungian theme came to be as we envisioned Anubis to be the one to guide us back to a sense of wholeness, to show us the Light and Dark, and to finally integrate the fragments of our Selves that have been scattered to the winds.

As He guides the Dead so shall He guide the living. He leads us back to a spiritual state of being and clears the mists from our minds so that we remember who we are. So many of us live a life that is a living death and need to be freed from that, BUT only if we are willing to change.

As Master of the Mysteries, it is Anubis who conducts the candidate across the threshold of the unseen world into the presence of terrifying apparitions and onwards through the twelve gates to Amenti for the final judgment. Anubis was an ancient funerary deity who was manifest in numerous guises and took many appellations but essentially remained the great god of the dead and lord of judgment in the afterlife. Alternatively, it very much depended upon which priesthood was in power!

At other times, Anubis took a human form but with the head of a jackal, which was worn as a mask by his priesthood during the funerary rites to symbolise the presence of the Neter, especially during the Opening of Mouth Ceremony.

Although maligned in some cultures as 'unclean', a comprehensive historical examination will demonstrate that few if any creatures have been as respected as the dog throughout history. Even more so when you consider the dog's wild predecessor, the wolf, as well as the dog itself. *Canis lupus* is currently classified by many scientists as the same species; therefore, it makes sense to analyse the history of the two species as one. Genetically, the dog is not even a subspecies of the wolf, but rather a separate species.

Within the covers of this book are amazing contributions from those who have both experienced Anubis and as a result, have their own story to tell.

This god has not been confined to the shores of Egypt and Europe but makes an appearance in Central and South America; a point which **Bill Duvendack** would like to discuss. Specifically, the connections and parallels between Anubis and the Aztec god of death, Mictlantecuhtli, as well as Xolotl. A great number of parallels between these three shed light on a piece of lost or forgotten history.

**Bob Trubshaw** discusses why the death-hound of Arthur Conan Doyle's *The Hound of the Baskervilles* is such a vigorous archetypal beast. Conan Doyle's inspiration was the folk tale of a phantom black dog on Dartmoor. In the Quantock Hills of Somerset, the black dog was frequently seen and called the 'Gurt Dog'. Cornwall has various tales of the 'Devil's Dandy (or Dando) Dogs', Devon has the 'Yeth (Heath) or Wisht Hounds'.

**Michael Starsheen** leads us through a pathworking, and we join him as he waits for a sign. The dark night is serene as the many sleep. The night begins to brighten, and birds begin to sing softly as dawn approaches. Anubis watched the horizon carefully, and finally, there it is! The bright, blue star, Sopdet, Star of Isis appears briefly on the horizon, only to be lost in the blare of the sunlight as Ra-Harakte rises on the last of the Epagomenal Days. Michael's words are set on a page like jewels.

**Dr. Tim Broussard** writes a chilling account of his initiatory process that reads more like a baptism of fire. His near-reality experience is not for the faint-hearted.

**Don Webb** has written a masterpiece of an Epilogue that sums up perfectly the 'being', and notion of the God Anubis.

What we will learn in this book is the magic of Anubis's darkness, the meaning of those shapes and Presence, as well as the light, change, healing, and strength that can arise from such knowledge. On magical levels, we will put dreary Osiris to rest at last, and restore his arch-rival, Anubis, to his proper place in all the worlds. On human levels, we will learn to awaken those forgotten or neglected parts of ourselves and become strong, magical beings.

ANUBIS ~ an INNER GUIDE

# PART I

# Origins

**Compiled by Judith Page**

Although we know him as Anubis, a name bestowed upon him by the Greeks, his Egyptian name was Anpu, Inpu, Anupu, Wip, or Inpw. The first recorded mention of the god Anubis may be found in documents from Egypt's Old Kingdom dating back to the third millennium BCE. The Old Kingdom is, as the name says, the earliest of the three ancient Egyptian kingdoms. The Middle Kingdom lasted from 2050 BC to 1800 BCE, whereas the New Kingdom lasted roughly from the sixteenth century BCE to the eleventh century BCE. The Old Kingdom is known best as the 'Age of the Pyramids' for the majority were constructed during that era.

The name has been the subject of various scholastic attempts for an etymological inference. Some have, with Set, theorised that the name means 'doggy'. Others have linked it to a word *inpw*, meaning 'royal child', or 'young prince', although the implications for such a connection are ambiguous.

In the Coffin Texts, a verb *inpw* appears with the meaning 'to decay', but Anubis' primary responsibility was of course to prevent decay. Finally, the hypothesis has been made that a verb *inpw* may have had the meaning, 'to lie down (on the stomach)'. If this were accurate, the name Anubis could mean 'the crouching one' which would really fit very perfectly.

When Anubis was mentioned in the Old Kingdom writings, it was in relation to the king's burial. He was known by several lengthy titles in ancient Egypt for his role as a funeral planner and in the deaths of Egyptians. Because of his epithet 'He who is atop his mountain', he has frequently been portrayed as the protector of tombs; a dog atop a building supposedly a tomb. He is the protector of the mountain, which is a tomb, or the many pyramids built in the Old Kingdom. He has another title that refers to his links to the mummification process describing him as 'He who is the area of embalming'. This title would liken Anubis to a supervisor, or overseer in the process of embalming the corpse.

Anubis takes on a variety of duties depending on specific roles, such as leading funerary processions or marches for other causes. This was shared by many other Egyptian deities; there was always an occasion to worship or give thanks for the tiny mercies they regarded as gifts from the gods. Anubis was shown in three different ways: totally human, fully canine, or with a human body and a canine head. While completely canine, he would be portrayed as a dog with a ribbon around his neck and a flail or whip held in the crook of one of his legs, perched on top of a tomb.

When Anubis is represented as a man, although this is rare, his skin is entirely black, as this colour is typically linked with death and funerals. As the jackal-headed man, he was linked with dogs, since Egyptians considered canines to be holy to the deceased.

Dogs were frequently observed near the edge of the desert where the Egyptians buried their dead. It is possible that people felt the dogs were guarding the deceased rather than digging up the bodies and devouring them.

The Anubis animal has been described as a jackal thus far. However, was this the case? Some people do not agree. There were three major canine divinities in ancient Egypt: Anubis, Khenti-Amentiu (from Abydos), and Wepwawet (from Assyut).

Wild dogs, jackals, wolves, and foxes are all candidates to become gods. Anubis was a dog, and Wepwawet was a wolf, according to the Greeks who often visited Egypt in the seventh century BCE. It's not clear what they thought about Khenti-Amentiu, as by the time the Greeks reached Egypt, Khenti-Amentiu had virtually ceased to exist as a separate god, and has become an epithet of Osiris instead.

The animals used to portray Anubis, Khenti-Amentiu or Wepwawet, are mostly indistinguishable from one another. They all show the same profile and the same colour, and they are all invariabley black. Wepwawet can be identified because he is always depicted upright on a standard with an mysterious object in front of him. In Sety 1st temple in Abydos he is portrayed with a white head. Khenti-Amentiu (illust.1) and Anubis are represented as recumbent. Unless their names are included in the image, there is no way to identify them.

**Influence In Egypt**
Later in Egyptian mythology, two belief frameworks merged: the Ogdoad and the Ennead system. We could consider it a fusion of Roman and Greek mythology, although in a more comparable dialect and with the same names. Following the merger of these systems, the god Osiris became the more prominent deity of the Underworld, while Anubis became more of a gatekeeper. Meanwhile, Osiris' religion flourished and prospered, and Anubis was granted Osiris' vital organs as a heavenly gift following his death at the hands of another divinity.

Anubis was appointed as a guardian of souls journeying to the Underworld, as well as a protector of lost souls. As a result, Anubis became the deity of orphans and the guardian of the process of passing from life to death.

After the burial ceremonies, he was depicted in the 'Opening of the Mouth' ceremony. Anubis clutched the soul and directed it away from the body, away from the living world, and into the land of the dead. He was represented as the weigher of the dead's heart since he was providing Osiris' critical organs.

# ANUBIS ~ an INNER GUIDE

While Anubis weighed the heart, he was accompanied by the supreme king of the Underworld, Osiris. In the presence of Djehuty, or Thoth, god of the moon, Anubis was the scribe of reckoning, learning, and writing, who communicated between the world of the gods and the world of the living. He measured the heart against the feather of truth, called 'Ma'at' and if falsehoods and crimes were heavier than Ma'at, man's soul would be punished. If the man's heart weighed the same as or less than the feather, the soul would go on. (illust.2)

Since Anubis had become the god of the dying rather than the god of the dead, he was merged as a deity with Upper Egypt's god of the dying.

**Anubis' Role and Relationship with Other Gods**
Anubis was the deity of the Underworld, the domain of death. In Egyptian mythology's original system, he was Ra's fourth son. Ra was a prominent deity in Egyptian mythology and the principal god of Heliopolis, which literally meant 'City of the Sun'. Although Ra was primarily the god of the sun, he also ruled over the sky, the earth, and the underworld. Because Egyptian monarchs, known as pharaohs, were considered to be the offspring of the Egyptian deity Ra, they were also

worshipped as gods. Anubis, on the other hand, was one of the first deities considered to be Ra's son. Later in Egyptian mythology, like Isis and Osiris, Nephthys and Set were married before birth. Though the marriage of Isis and Osiris was full of love, Nephthys and Set's relationship was not.

In later traditions, Nephthys had an affair with Osiris and gave birth to his son Anubis. Fearing that Set would discover her infidelity, Nephthys abandoned her child in the wilderness.

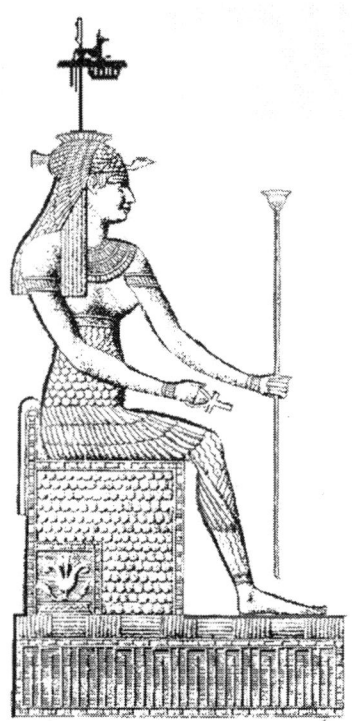

Anput (Input) was the wife of Anubis, the mother of Kebechet (the goddess of purification) and the personification of the seventeenth Nome of Upper Egypt. Her name is merely the female version of the name of her husband, Anubis ('t' is the feminine ending and Anubis was known as Anpu or Inpu to the Egyptians). (illust. 3)

Anubis was also said to have another wife, the goddess of icy water, Neheb Kau, Nehebka, Kebechet or Kebauet. In other parts of Egypt, Kebechet was represented as his daughter. She was also the principal female deity of the cleansing of bodily organs before they were placed in their ceremonial jars and kept alongside the body during the process of mummification, or embalming.

Anubis' major duty was to embalm the dead. He was also alleged to be the tutor of those who did the actual mummification. High priests performed the embalming process while wearing the mask

of the deity Anubis, the head of a dog. Anubis is also supposed to be his father Osiris' embalmer, maki.ng him Horus' older brother.

In ancient Egyptian lore, there are two divine beings that share the 'Horus' name. Horus the Elder, also known as Horus the Great, was the fourth of the five gods to be born to Nut and Geb. Their names were Osiris, Isis, Nephthys, Horus (the Elder) and Set. (illust. 4)

Horus the Younger was the son born to Isis and Osiris. Some academics say that Horus the Elder and Horus the Younger are different forms of the same god, whilst others say they are two separate gods. At some point, both gods Older and Younger merged into one and mostly symbolised the deity of the sky and rulers.

**Dog City**
That the Greeks referred to Hardai as Cynopolis, or 'Dog City,' reveals how they saw this deity in their minds. Dogs were mummified and deposited in the Anubis temples during Roman times. Dog cemeteries in the city of Hardai make it evident that this god was sometimes linked with domestic canines, as well.

While the Greeks called the Anubis sacred city Cynopolis, the city of Wepwawet was known as Lycopolis (Delta) 'Wolf City.' The original king of the dead before Osiris took that position, Wepwawet was intimately connected with Egyptian royalty. According to Egyptian mythology, Wepwawet, the Lord of the Dead, was the King of Kings, and his original glory has been preserved on two of the four royal standards.

The king's standard, known as the *'shedshed'* or, *'bundle of life'*, held the royal placenta, and adorned with a picture of Wepwawet it was used to lead Pharaoh's forces into war. Additionally, it was expected, upon the death of Pharaoh, to accompany him to the afterlife. Wepwawet's personal standard signified Upper Egypt, the unity of the two countries, and the Egyptian nobility. (illust. 5)

But, like Anubis, he was an earlier Egyptian deity, the oldest of Abydos, the birthplace of Egypt's first dynasty. His principal associations after relinquishing the title of Lord of the Dead to Osiris were kingship, war, and the unification rituals, but he retained funeral importance.

As with Anubis, Wepwawet is often shown as a wolf, hound, or jackal, as well as an apparent hybrid between these animals.

Set was another deity who often took the shape of a dog. Set's popularity waned throughout time, despite his status as an old deity. As the god of the desert and storm, he is perhaps most remembered for his feud with the god of the underworld, Osiris, and Horus, his son. Set was often shown as a dog, although he is depicted as a variety of creatures and even a person with an aardvark's head. There is a depiction of him as a greyhound in one hieroglyph variation of his name.

In the beginning, Set was equal to Osiris, but as the fame of Osiris and his son Horus grew, Set became eviller. In Lower Egypt, he served as a symbol until he became the patron deity of the invading Hyksos. He set himself up as a devil-like figure after the Hyksos were expelled from Egypt.

Though he is most often linked with the ibis and baboon, Djehuty (Thoth), god of the moon, sacred texts, mathematics, the sciences, magic, messenger, and recorder of the deities, master of knowledge, and patron of scribes, Thoth may also appear as a baboon with a dog's head.

**How Anubis is perceived by Non-Egyptians**

At one point in time, Greek mythology merged with that of the ancient Egyptians. The gods of ancient Egypt and the Greeks produce new gods that would ultimately be disregarded in favour of the Greek pantheon of gods that is recognisable to many today. This happened during the Ptolemaic era, when the Greeks designated Hermes as the messenger of the gods. The two faiths and mythologies blended, and Anubis and Hermes became one god. Hence, this period gave rise to a god dressed in Grecian apparel with a dog's head and given the name 'Hermanubis'. (illust. 6)

It's no secret that the Greeks were not enamoured with Egyptian customs and beliefs. In certain cultures, the veneration of dogs was on par with that of demons. The Greeks referred to Anubis as 'the Barker' because of their scorn for the Egyptian gods.

Another reason why the Greeks and Romans disliked Egyptian deities such as Anubis was the widespread belief that dogs are scavengers of the dead. Because of their lowly status, they were compared to the maggots that feasted on decaying flesh. Despite Tertillian's criticism of Egyptian religion, he and others disregarded the maggot's mission. Scavengers like crows, worms, and even dogs help keep the living alive by cleaning the carcasses of their prey. In a metaphorical sense, the same may be stated.

The surviving will slacken off even quicker if they don't pay proper respects to the deceased. But despite the Greeks evident disdain and even dread, they still associated Anubis with the star Sirius in the sky and with Cerberus in the underworld.

Sirius appears in many guises in myth. Robertino Solàrion's article taken from Robert Temple's, *The Sirius Mystery* is a worthy account. Plutarch described Anubis as a 'horizontal circle, which divides the unseen portion... which they call Nephthys, from the visible portion... which they call Isis; and as this circle touches the boundaries of both light and darkness, it can be viewed as shared by both.'

This appears to be a clear description of an ancient account of a circular orbit (named 'Anubis') of a dark and invisible star (called 'Nephthys') around its sister,' a light and visible star (called 'Isis') – and we know Isis was identified with Sirius or Sobdet by the ancient Egyptians. What is missing here are the following precise points, which must be our assumptions at this stage: (a) The circle represents an orbit. (b) In this sense, the divine characters are literally stars. (illust. 7: Sobdet, tomb of Seti 1st)

Sometimes Osiris and Anubis were confused for one another. It is fair and expected that Osiris, the companion of Isis who is occasionally referred to as "the companion of Sirius," would be associated with the orbit of the latter.

Sirius, also known as the Dog-Star, is the brightest star in the constellation Canis Major. The pre-dawn rising of the star in the path of the sun was believed to be the source of the scorching heat and droughts of midsummer.

## The Dog in Egypt

When researching the dog, few historical records are older than those of the ancient Egyptians. According to the testimony of the ancient Greeks, the Egyptians loved dogs and treated them with great respect. Dogs received burial in family tombs and family members would shave their heads in mourning at the death of a family dog.

Even in the predynastic period, we see that the Egyptians were already burying dogs in the same way they buried humans, with plenty of goods for the afterlife. In dynastic Egypt, dog mummies were made with great care and expense. At Hardai, the sacred city of the god Anubis there are sprawling cemeteries.

When thinking of dogs as deities few come to mind as quickly as Anubis (aka Anpu). While sometimes represented clearly as a dog, at other times he appears more like a jackal.

The most common representation of Anubis appears like a cross between a dog, a jackal and a wolf. The same image is commonly used to portray Wepwawet. This has led some to believe that the Egyptians may have interbred domestic dogs with the wild dogs of Egypt, in particular the jackal and wolf.

Note: The Nomes of Egypt retained their primary importance as administrative units until the fundamental rearrangement of the bureaucracy during the reigns of Diocletian and Constantine the Great.

##  Animism ~ Totemism Fetishism to God

### Compiled by Judith Page

The Egyptian god Anubis is not a jackal at all, but a member of the wolf family. In fact, researchers believe the animal is older than the well-known wolves of the northern hemisphere.

**We begin with animism**
The gods are the children of adoration. However, their genealogy reaches back into the past. Early peoples, unable to differentiate between living and inanimate forms, thought that each item around them, like themselves, was embedded with life.

All living things, including trees, winds, and rivers, have life and consciousness. Trees moan and rustle as if they are speaking, or perhaps they are the home of mighty spirits. The winds are brimming with words, sighing, warnings, threats, and, without a doubt, the sounds of roaming forces or entities, both friendly and unfriendly. The water in rivers and seas is moving, articulating, and prophesying. Even abstract features were meant to have living-like characteristics. The heat and cold were considered active and alert agents for light and darkness. The sky was regarded as the Father from whom all living things had arisen as a result of his collaboration with Mother Earth. Animism is the term for this type of belief system.

**Next, we move on to totemism**
It is interesting to note that a considerable number of people and places in the Old Testament have names derived from animals.

Zeeb, the wolf, princes of the Midianites, and Zeboim the hyena. Many of these, however, are personal names; but among the Israelite tribes mentioned in Numbers 26, are the Shualites, or fox clan of Asher. Other tribes having similar names are Calebites or dog tribes.

It was thought that if inanimate objects and natural occurrences were imbued with the attributes of life and consciousness, the creatures of the animal world were elevated to a higher realm.

In each of these attributes the several animals to whom they belonged appeared to the native as more gifted than himself, and so deeply was he influenced by this seeming superiority that if he coveted a certain quality, he would place himself under the protection of the animal or bird which symbolised it.

Again, if a tribe or clan possessed any special characteristic, such as fierceness or cunning, it was usually called by its neighbours after the bird or beast which signified its character.

This belief is known as totemism, and its adoption was the means of laying the foundation of a widespread system of tribal rule and custom, by which marriage and many of the affairs of life were and are wholly governed. Probably all European and Asiatic peoples have passed through this stage, and its remains are to be found deeply embedded in social systems.

**The dog as ancestor and totem**
The veneration of dog ancestry and totems is quite widespread but especially prevalent in eastern Asia and North America. The wolf appears on the totem poles of many Amerindian tribes along the Pacific coast. When this happens, killing a wolf or eating its flesh is prohibited. The sacrifice of a totem can, however, be used instead as a religious ceremony.

A new study by Peter Savolainen and others suggests that all domestic dogs evolved from a few maternal lineages somewhere in eastern Asia. This notion is interesting. Savolainen also proposes that the ancestor of the dingo, now found throughout Southeast Asia and Australia, was transported by Austronesian speakers some 6,000 years ago.

One of the more significant Bantu ethnic groups in southern Africa, the Xhosa, trace their ancestry back to a dog. The Kyrgyz, the Nicobarese, the Pomotu islands, and other groups in Papua New Guinea, Myanmar, and as far away as Finland have also maintained such beliefs.

Jonica Newby, author of *Animal Attraction*, a history of animal domestication, suggests that dingoes might represent an early domestic dog and the closest progenitor to all dogs. Rather than deriving from the Indian Canis lupus pallipes, the dingo could have descended from Canis lupus chanco, an East Asian subspecies of the Grey Wolf.

When it comes to canine deities, it's common to see them depicted as being married to a goddess, or, as in South China's case, to a daughter of the Chinese Emperor. Hmong, Mien, and other ethnic groups in South China and northern Indochina are well-known for their belief in these myths.

In the Mien version of the narrative, Chinese Emperor Pien Hung faces defeat at the hands of Emperor Kao Wang and promises his daughter to anyone who can fight the invader. Hearing this, the three-coloured dog, Phan Hu, penetrates enemy lines, kills Kao Wang, and returns his head to Pien Hung. Taking the emperor's daughter as his wife, they have twelve offspring, from whom the Mien clans are descended. The children despised life in metropolitan China and sought sanctuary in South China's lush mountain regions.

Fetishism is a third form of belief that thrives alongside animism and totemism. This comes from the Portuguese word 'feitigo', which means 'manufactured charm', and is used to describe any item, great or small, natural or manmade, that is thought to have awareness, volition, or supernatural attributes, notably 'orienda', or magical power.

While the majority of authors agree that the word fetish comes from the Portuguese, feitigo, which is derived from the Latin, factitius, current opinions on what fetishism is varies, and in some cases, is completely contradictory. There is no question that there are other types of fetishism, but some academics such as E. B. Taylor define fetishism as 'the idea of spirits embedded in, or connected to, or transmitting influences through, specific material items' that serve as 'vessels, vehicles, or instruments of spiritual beings.'

All things, including animals, water, the soil, trees, stones, celestial bodies, and even night and day, as well as characteristics such as light and darkness, were thought to have liveliness and the ability to choose. This might imply anything bad, such as being possessed by a spell.

Natives believed the rocks and the trees to be living tombs of imprisoned spirits, resembling the dryads of Greek folklore, so it is not difficult for them to imagine an intelligence, potent, in any object, no matter how unusual. The more unusual the object, the greater the probability of it being in the abode of some powerful intelligence, incarcerated for revenge or for some other reason. In short, the leap to items with fetish force is a typical human leap.

Karl Marx (5 May 1818 - 14 March 1883) famously observed that relations between people in capitalist society assume the form of relations between things. The fetishism of money and commodities thus obscures the social foundation of these objects as a result of the alienating split between people and the products of their labour. It simultaneously animates such things, by attributing to them autonomous value, productivity, or growth.

Goblet d'Alviella (*Hibbert Lectures*, London, 1891) defines fetishism as the *'belief that the appropriation of a thing may secure the services of the spirit lodged within it'*. And an object becomes a fetish when spirits penetrate into it, and so make it the vehicle or organ of their own personality. He carefully distinguishes between the talisman or amulet and the fetish, for in the former the spirits act on inanimate things from without, using them as implements, while in the latter the spirits are embodied in a concrete object. On African fetishism see Nassau, *Fetishism in West Africa*, London, 1904. This work contains the best and fullest account of West African Fetishism which has hitherto appeared.

Although there are hundreds of Egyptian gods and goddesses that could be discussed in this chapter, we will only be referring to those with canine associations.

The earliest documented image of a *jmy-wt* fetish may be seen on the handle of a Predynastic jug dating back to the Naqada II period. This particular handle purports to show the process by which intestines were removed from a sacrificial bird and tied to the fetish.

Throughout the reigns of the kings Hor-Aha, Djer, Djet, and Den of the First Dynasty, the fetish is shown on seals and labels. During this time period, the *jmy-wt* is connected with the ritualised execution of prisoners. (illust. 8)

Another example was discovered in 1914 by an expedition of the Metropolitan Museum of Art near the pyramid of Senusret 1st and was housed in a shrine at the time of its discovery.

There are images of the *jmy-wt* fetish on the walls of ancient Egyptian temples, and copies of it were sometimes included with funerary accoutrements, most notably the two that Howard Carter discovered in the tomb of Tutankhamun. These emblems of Anubis were placed at the western ends of the corridors, one on each side of the outermost shrine. The fetish itself was gilded, and the pots were made of Egyptian alabaster.

Around the Fourth Dynasty, the fetish became associated with the god Anubis and mummification, therefore it is also referred to as the Anubis fetish. (illust. 9)

Thomas Logan suggests that the *jmy.wt* has its origin as a standard associated with kingship and transition, a pole upon which the intestines of a ritual animal sacrifice were hung. This he connects to an etymology *jmy.wt* 'that which is inside', analogous to *jmyw* 'tumour'. In this scenario, the name was later re-analysed as a reference to embalming - after the association with Anubis.

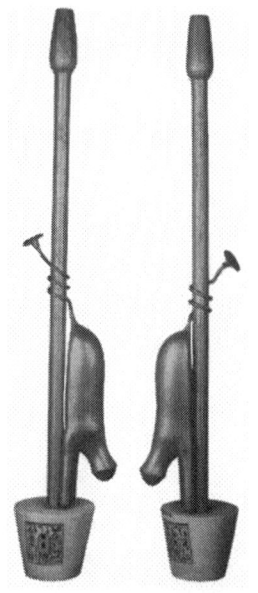

This was a religious object symbolised by a stuffed and headless animal hide attached to a pole that depicted the water lily (lotus) stem and bud, and the tip of the skin's tail had a papyrus blossom attached. (illust.10)

This fetish was a depiction of a person during the burial ceremonies presided over by Anubis. Although the *jmy-wt* has been documented throughout the history of ancient Egypt and appears in the oldest

Egyptian mythological records, there are insufficient documents to identify exactly what sort of deity *jmy-wt* actually was.

There is proof of this fetish dating back to the 1st Dynasty and is known as the 'Son of the Hesat-Cow' (the cow that produced the Mer-wer bull associated with the cow goddess Hesat). They had ties to the funerary cult, which was represented in the Chapel of Anubis in Hatshepsut's mortuary temple. (illust. 11)

Fetishes constructed of real animal skin wrapped in bandages have also been unearthed. 'He Who is in His Wrappings' (Imiut), the god of early times became the form of Anubis. Although it appears to have also been connected to the Heb Sed Festival, the fetish was most likely associated with the wrappings used for mummified bodies.

*Anubis the Dweller in the Mummy Chamber, Governor of the Divine House ... saith:- 'Homage to thee, thou happy one, lord!*
*Thou seest the Utchat. Ptah-Seker hath bound thee up. Anubis hath exalted thee.*
*Shu hath raised thee up, O Beautiful Face, thou governor of eternity.*
*Thou hast thine eye, O scribe Nebseni, lord of fealty, and it is beautiful.*
*Thy right eye is like the Sektet Boat, thy left eye is like the Atet Boat.*
*Thine eyebrows are fair to see in the presence of the Company of the Gods.*
*Thy brow is under the protection of Anubis, and thy head and face, O beautiful one, are before the holy Hawk.*
*Thy fingers have been established by thy scribe's craft in the presence of the Lord of Khemenu, Thoth, who hath bestowed upon thee the knowledge of the speech of the holy books.*
*Thy beard is beautiful in the sight of Ptah-Seker, and thou, O scribe*

*Nebseni, thou lord of fealty, art beautiful before the Great Company of the Gods.*
*The Great God looketh upon thee, and he leadeth thee along the path of happiness.*
*Sepulchral meals are bestowed upon thee, and he overthroweth for thee thine enemies, setting them under thy feet in the presence of the Great Company of the Gods who dwell in the House of the Great Aged One which is in Anu.'* (illust. 12)
[The Speech of Anubis from the Papyrus of Nu and the Papyrus of Nebseni[

Note: Although its origin and purpose is unknown, one idea is that it represented a sacrificial animal, the ritual killings of prisoners, or that it symbolises Anubis as an embalmer. In some instances, the *imiut* was thought to be a deity, perhaps representing the flayed skin of the god Nemty. In other images, it is a symbol of Osiris. One theory, is that the *imiut* originally was supposed to be a bloody leopard skin. One account recorded in the first millennium B.C.E. tells how the god Set, disguising himself as a leopard, set about to defile the body of Osiris. Anubis apprehended him, and branded the god all over with a hot iron. According to Egyptian myth, this is how the leopard got its spots. After flaying Set, Anubis wore his bloody skin as a deterrent to all those intent on disturbing the dead. Anubis decreed that priests should wear leopard skins to honour his triumph over Set.

# How He was Usurped

**Compiled by Judith Page**

It must be pointed out that the first God of Abydos and god of the dead, Khenti-Amentiu, was represented as a sitting dog – similar to the Set animal – and was renowned as the 'protector of the necropolis'. His name suggests 'first of the westerners' or 'first of the dead', which is ironic because this deity in its animal form was able to dig up and destroy corpses. It clearly demonstrates its dominance over them and, as a result, appears fit to be entrusted with their protection.

The name Khenti-Amentiu appears on the necropolis cylinder seals for the 1st Dynasty Pharaohs, Den and Qa'a, naming each of their predecessors with the title 'Horus Khenti-Amentiu', starting with 'Horus Khenti-Amentiu Narmer'. (Illust. 13)

He is one of those dog-shaped gods who have surfaced as necropolis gods in many locations. Canides has become a generic word for the entire family, including Set, making zoological identification difficult. As a result, outside of Abydos, all the dog-headed gods are commonly referred to as Anubis - Anubis Lord of the Caverns; Anubis Lord of the White Lands, which connects to Set's territory, the desert.

But it is Abydos that has been celebrated for almost three thousand years as the primary centre of worship of the dog-god Khenti-Amentiu. Due to the holiness of the place, many Egyptian kings were buried there, even as early as the end of the fourth and beginning of the third millennium, and the custom continued into the second century BCE.

In the 1st Dynasty, a temple dating back to pre-dynastic times was built for this god just beyond the town of Abydos. It was fashioned in reeds very much on the lines of one in Nekhen (City of the Hawk, or City of the Falcon, a reference to Horus) (illust. 14)

It consisted of a temple proper for the deity and a slaughtering enclosure to the northwest. There was a sanctuary at the heart of the temple surrounded by two adjoining side rooms. The design was such, that the exterior structure could be expanded multiple times.

The slaughtering enclosure was used to prepare sacrifices for the departed king as well as for Khenti-Amentiu, the dog-god.

The slaughtering enclosure was an integral feature of the temple and was accessible from the procession road on the left side, where it led to the royal cemetery through another gate. When a loved one died, mourners would leave small pots in the desert as a tribute. (illust. 15)

The present name for this cemetery is Umm el Qa'ab, which means 'Mother of Pots', because the entire region is covered with shattered pot shards from previous offerings. A procession from the cultivated land would have to pass by the protective deity's home, and the passing by was obviously associated with the god's ritual visitation and deeds aimed at securing his protection. Illust. 16 & 17)

Abydos soon became a place of pilgrimage for devout Egyptians, whose wish beyond all else was to be buried as close as possible to Abydos. Of course, this was not possible for many due to the expense, so instead, stelae were set up inscribed with the dead person's name and titles. Donations were given to the priesthood for prayers to be said to the god.

Small figures that may have come from the Khenti-Amentiu temple were uncovered in a pit-type storeroom near these ruins. They include images of monkeys, frogs, hippopotami, crocodiles, and birds, as well as votive figures that were delivered to the temple of the god of the dead. The supplicants may have asked the god for physical fertility. Monkeys could be a reference to the king's death. The ancients believed that the dead could bring about fertility and progeny.

The town of Abydos at the time had no importance, it had little bearing on politics or history, and did not serve as the regional capital. But its true significance resided in the fact that it was the product of two distinct practices: the enduring funerary cult of the earlier pharaohs and the worship of an imported deity known as Ws'r, or Osiris. Toby Wilkinson, Egyptologist, and author, suggests that, even at this early stage, Khenti-Amentiu's name may have been simply an epithet of Ws'r.

All of this would not have been enough to save the two distinct cults of Abydos—the royal burial ceremony and the associated cult of the temple of Khenti-Amentiu's—had it not been for the deity Osiris, who seemed to be the heavenly embodiment of a fundamental aspect of Egyptian religion. Since Ws'r/Osiris was an imported god who reached an almost historic and mythological amalgamation of his multifaceted nature, the sacred Abydos sites did not become a historical remembrance of an ancient dog-god but rather timeless ever-present importance.

We need to peel back many layers of growth to that time when, as far as we are aware, the region had historical significance, new forms of belief, and practices of worship. Only then will we be able to fully understand this phenomenon. As a result, the location retained its special significance and remained a significant centre of religious activity.

Let us look briefly at the nature of this god known as W'sr or Osiris. We need to think about where he came from and why he became so revered, so much so, that his importance eventually spread far beyond the borders of Egypt. Ramesses IV's described his character as being more perplexing than other gods', and this still holds true today. Academics still disagree about him, and the following is therefore only an attempt to trace the history of the god and to say something about his nature. Especially as far as his supposed origins are concerned.

On one hand Osiris is grouped with the Near Eastern gods of resurrection, and similar images of him have been discovered in Eridu, the city of the god Enki dating back to the Ubaid period. On the other hand, he is supposed to have been a prehistoric chieftain or monarch who lived who later became a deity.

Osiris represented the spiritual authority of a 'dweller in the underworld', as described in ancient texts. As a result of this, corn and other crops are able to grow out of the soil, and this has a tight relationship to the energy manifested during the flooding of the Nile. Even if it's not exactly the same thing as a force, the earth provides a sort of home and living place, just as does the Nile.

To appreciate this force, one has to think of it as a human being according to ancient perceptions. When man makes a statement about God, God must take on human characteristics. In keeping with Egyptian conceptions of heaven and earth, this chthonic power of fertility should be depicted as a male creature. Ancient Egyptians, unlike most Semitic civilizations, always viewed the earth as a masculine being, both grammatically and religiously. It was just a matter of time before the sky became a woman for them. An Egyptian woman's fertile womb was unimaginable. Plants are thought to grow 'on the back of Geb', which is a male reclining on the ground with the feminine sky (Nut) leaning over him (the earth god). No evidence exists that the god of chthonic fertility had the name Osiris when he was first shown. There is no record of him from that time period. In contrast, it is impossible to explain the name Osiris in a convincing manner. (illust. 18)

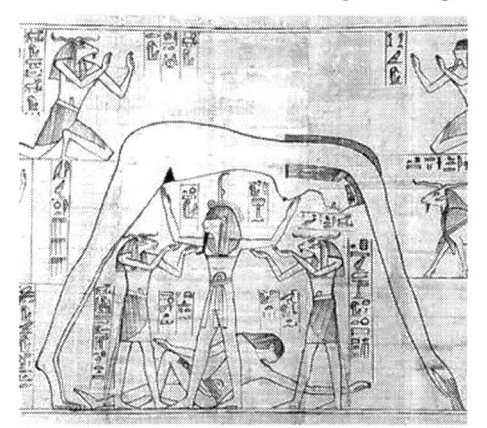

# Opening of the Mouth Ceremony

**Compiled by Judith Page**

The intention of the ceremonies and spells was the rebuilding the body of the dead man and restoring the heart-soul, Ba, and the double, Ka. At the moment of death, spiritual elements, unimportant to man, left him, but the immortal spirit-soul, the Khu, went to the home of the spirit souls beyond the limits of this world and commonly termed heaven. The heart-soul and the ka remained on earth close to the body and would always be provided with sustenance in the form of meat and drink, as well as a dwelling place.

The ritual called The Opening of the Mouth ceremony was designed to re-animate the deceased and was important in both funerary and temple practice. Originally, the ceremony was performed on the actual dead body, but subsequently, due to a change of belief, a statue was substituted for it. The aim was to endow statues with the ability to support the living ka, and to receive offerings. It was performed on cult statues, on kings, and on private individuals, as well as on mummies of both humans and the sacred Apis bulls. The ceremony was even carried out on the individual rooms of temples and indeed on the entire temple structure.

Earliest references to The Opening of the Mouth ceremony come from the Pyramid Texts, inscribed on the burial chamber of the pyramid of Unas, dating to the end of the 5th Dynasty. One set of texts referring to the use of the fingers to open the mouth is in Pyramid Texts 1329–1330, translated by Raymond O. Faulkner as:
*'your mouth is split open by Horus with this little finger of his with which he split open the mouth of his father Osiris.'*

Besides the fingers, other implements were added, as indicated by Spells 11–15 of the Pyramid Texts. They describe The Opening of the Mouth ceremony using the foreleg of a bull and an adze (iron wood-working tool). Other inscriptions state an offering ritual in which two blades of meteoric iron, called the *ntjrwy*, are said to open the mouth. Faulkner translates this spell as:

*'O Osiris the King, I split open your mouth for you gods iron of Upper Egypt, 1 ingot; gods iron of Lower Egypt, 1 ingot.'*

The earliest complete version of the Opening of the Mouth ceremony dates to the 19th Dynasty embodied in a drawn-out ceremony performed at funerals in or in front of the tomb. King Sety 1st had one such scene portrayed on his tomb, as did the Grand Vizier Rekhmire who held office under both Tuthmosis III and Amenhotep II. These painted scenes are among the finest on the subject.

As already mentioned, in the earliest times the ceremonies were performed on the actual dead body, but subsequently, due to a change of belief, a statue was substituted for it. This statue was set upon a mound of sand in the House of Gold, with its face turned towards the south. Why the statue should be placed with its face towards the south is not stated, but we can assume that the orientation of the statue in this direction was in accordance with belief, or tradition, from remote antiquity.

A Kher-heb, chief priest, would recite the prescribed methods as he scattered the sand over the mound. The heaping of sand to form a foundation for the statue was an important part of the ceremony. It had to be performed with due care and devotion, as it was believed to impart sacredness or holiness.

At a point in the preceding, the chief priest declared that the heart-soul and kha had entered the abode of the statue, and the funeral feast then took place.

It is interesting to note that after the site of a temple had been marked out, it was the custom to scatter sand over it in order to sanctify the building to be erected upon it; this act spiritually strengthened its foundations.

The actual ritual consisted of many acts, with the opening of the mouth being just one. The first part was the ablution or washing of the mummy that had been set up on the mound of sand. The water had to be purified with water poured from *nmst* and *dshrt* jars, and the mummy's mouth especially was purified with balls of natron from Upper and Lower Egypt.

The mummy was then fumigated by incense. This part of the purification goes back to the Pyramid Texts, spells 16–29 where perfume is used. At this time, the Shem priest was awakened and prepared and dressed in his ceremonial leopard skin. The Shem priest opened the statue's mouth with his fingers rather than with the adze. (illust 19 & 20)

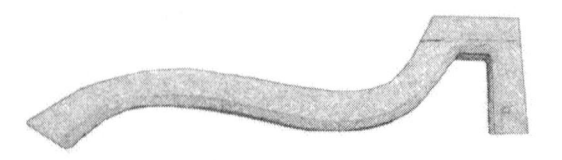

*Wooden Adze*

The hearts of bulls, Bull of Amentet, would have been torn out from their bodies, and the foreleg (shape of Ursa Major and adze) which had been cut off from each, was presented to the deceased. The hieroglyph for foreleg denoted strength and was considered to have transferred the life force of the bull to the recipient of the Opening of the Mouth (alternatively, the bull may have had the meaning of reviving sexual powers). The spirits of these offerings were intended to be the food of the gods, and the doubles and their heart-souls, and the material elements in the incarnate Osiris were eaten by the officiating priests, together with the relatives of the deceased. Eating the offerings of the dead, entered them into communion with the spiritual beings of the Other World. Osiris was seen to be the victim and deliverer, and the food of the souls of the dead and of the living. Does this remind you of another ritual?

In addition to the bulls, particular types of geese and gazelle were slain, and their bodies were also presented to the dead. These animals were regarded as the incarnations of the enemies of Osiris, who were captured at some remote period by the servants of the god, and brought and slain before him. The god consumed these spirits, and their bodies were eaten by his followers. (illust. 21)

*Mourners ~ Tomb of Khonsu, Gourna*

The ancient Egyptians believed that rituals existed that would bring sensory life back to the deceased's body, enabling it to see, smell, breathe, hear and eat and therefore partake of the offering of food and drink brought to the tomb each day. Priests would recite hymns such as the one for Pa-nefer:

*'Awake!..May you be alert as a living one, rejuvenated every day, healthy in millions of occasions of god sleep, while the gods protect you, protection being around you every day.'*

The principal ceremonies described were practiced among the Pre-dynastic Egyptians of the later part of the Neolithic Period, a fact verified by the flint Peshen-kef instrument now in the British Museum. It would appear that these ceremonies were performed mostly at Abydos in a time before the Egyptians learned or evolved the art of writing, and certainly precede the time and association of Osiris with this area.

During the IIIrd and IVth Dynasty, and the development of the cult of Osiris, new ceremonies and methods were added to the old, and even under the Ancient Empire the ceremony of the Opening the Mouth became virtually a replication of the performances and words narrated by the Sons of Horus for Osiris, his father. (illust.22)

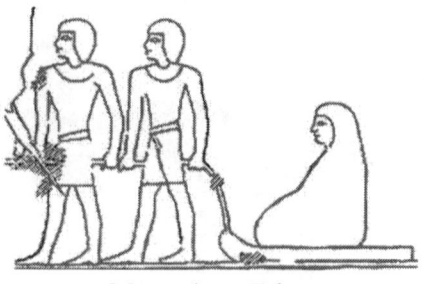

*Mysterious Tekenu*

The cult of the ancestor god was widespread in Sudan and in Egypt right up to the beginning of the Dynastic Period and merged with the cult of Osiris, the living/dead Man-god, and the ceremony endured in this form substantively until the beginning of the Roman Period.

1 ~ Slaughtering of the bull
2 ~ Sem priest presents the thigh to Pharaoh
3 ~ Sem priest presents the thigh to Pharaoh
4 ~ Sem priest presents the Seb-hur
5 ~ Sem priest addressing Pharaoh in the presence of a Kher-Heb

6 ~ Sem priest opens the mouth of Pharaoh with the needle of iron made of *smu* metal
7 ~ Sem priest presents Pharaoh with a cone of incense
8 ~ Sem priest utters: 'You have come into Purification'
9 ~ Sem priest offers four boxes

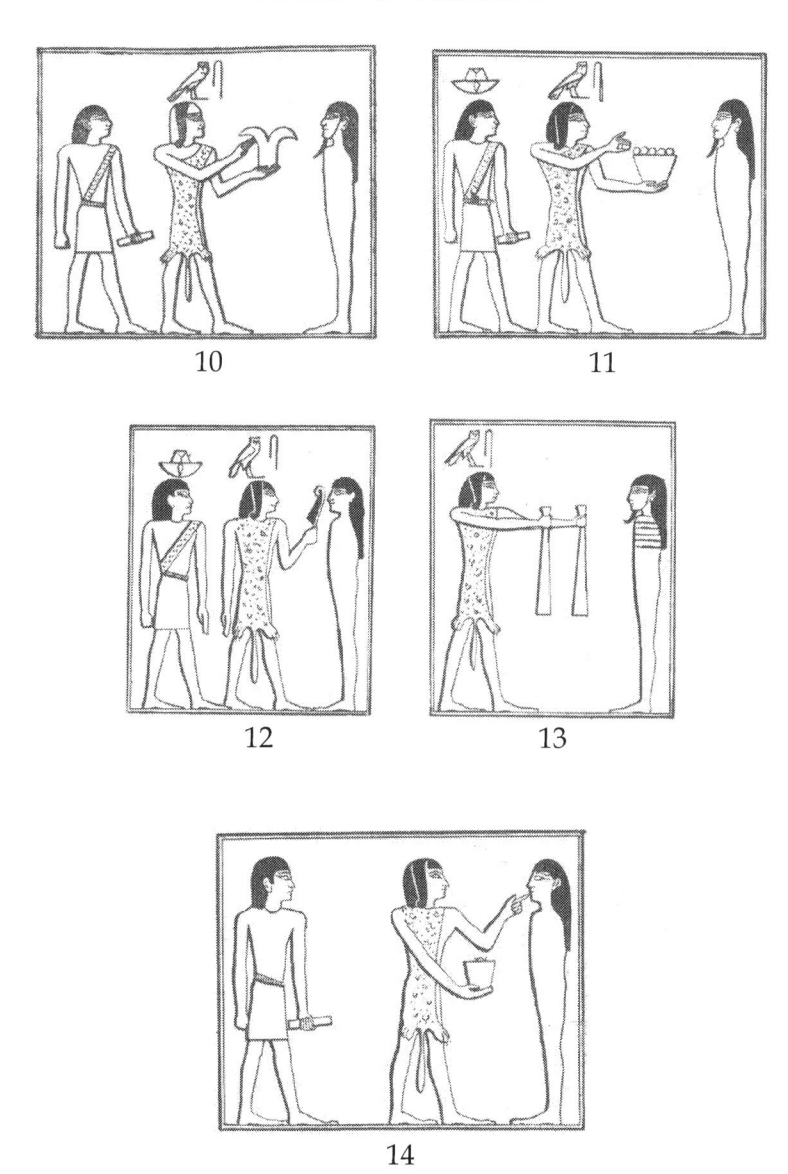

10 ~ Sem priest lays the Peshen-Kef on Pharaoh's lips
11 ~ Sem priest places grapes on Pharaoh's mouth
12 ~ Sem priest waves the Tunt-tet in front of Pharaoh's mouth and eyes
13 ~ Sem priest presents the Nemes Bandet
14 ~ Sem priest anoints Pharaoh with *uatch* and *mestchem*

# What is the Book of the Dead?

**Compiled by Judith Page**

Today, the Egyptians call these spells 'the Book of the Dead,' a modern term for an ancient collection of Egyptian magic spells that helped them enter the afterlife. Those who believed in the afterlife envisioned it as a dangerous journey that required magical assistance to complete. The ancient Egyptian religion taught that people had to undergo trials after death as they proceeded toward the underworld.

Unlike the Bible or any other collection of theory or statements of faith, the Book of the Dead is a practical guide to the hereafter, complete with spells to aid in your travels.

Many of these spells are written in hieroglyphic script on rolls of papyrus, which is what is commonly referred to as the 'book.' Papyrus rolls are often adorned with beautifully coloured illustrations. These were costly and would have only been available to the well-off and influential. According to how much money one had to spend, one could either buy an already made-up papyrus, which would have blank places for one's name, or one could spend a little more and select the spells they wanted.

Some of the spells were designed to ensure that the person would be able to govern their own body when they died. It was feared by the ancient Egyptians that a person's body, spirit, name, and heart would all disperse when a person died. Many spells were available to ensure that they didn't lose their mind or heart, that their body wouldn't decompose, and that they would continue to breathe, drink, and eat.

In addition to protection charms, ancient Egyptians anticipated being attacked by snakes, crocodiles, and insects on their journey to the afterlife, a belief that was based on the real-life hazards they understood but was considerably more terrifying and lethal.

In addition to the animals, the deceased may also have been assaulted by gods or demons who served the gods. To enter the next realm, it was necessary to pass a number of gods who defended the gateways, and if the person could not answer their questions correctly these gods would attack with knives and snakes in their hands.

With no protection spells, one could face the slaughter block, face decapitation, or be flipped upside down (which meant you would consume your own fæces for the rest of your afterlife!) There were many ways to be punished if one lacked the right protection spells.

That which was called the 'second death' was the most dreaded. As a result, you were pronounced dead, and your spirit was unable to return, leaving you with no hope for resurrection. The Book of the Dead served as a guide and a shield for those who made their way into the underworld.

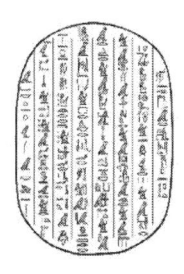

It sheds light on the ancient Egyptians' intricate beliefs about death and the afterlife, which were at the heart of their civilisation. Even though the term is well-known today, the mystical visuals and texts are actually far more extensive than is commonly thought. Illustrations depicting the fields and rivers of the underworld, the gods and demons the deceased would meet, and the critical 'weighing of the heart' ritual, sheds light on the ancient Egyptians' intricate beliefs about death and the afterlife, which were at the heart of their civilisation. (illust. 24). Even though the term is well-known today, the mystical visuals and texts are actually far more extensive than is commonly thought. Illustrations depicting the fields and rivers of the underworld, the gods and demons the deceased would meet, and the critical 'weighing of the heart' ritual, that determined whether or not the soul was accepted into heaven or condemned to eternal damnation at the hands of the monstrous 'Devourer', are a visual enlightenment.

Chapters 30 and 125 of the Book of Coming Forth by Day, as well as the Weighing of the Heart, provide classic examples of judgement at death. When it comes to wisdom and memory in ancient Egypt, it wasn't believed to be in the brains but rather in the heart, or ib. The heart was regarded as the most significant of the internal organs because of its apparent ties to the intellect, personality, and memories. After death, one's true self may be seen through the heart's reflection in the body, according to this concept, hence it was left in the body during mummification.

A second trial was that the deceased would have to recite a negative confession *'when [she or] he descends to the hall of the Two Truths.'* In the statement, he or she swore that they had *not* engaged in specific behaviours while alive. According to Ahmed Osman, author about ancient Egypt, one translation of the statement reads:
*'Hail to thee, great God, Lord of the Two Truths. I have come unto thee, my Lord, that thou mayest bring me to see thy beauty. I know thee, I know thy name, I know the names of the 42 Gods who are with thee in this broad hall of the Two Truths . . . Behold, I am come unto thee. I have brought thee truth; I have done away with sin for thee.*
*I have not sinned against anyone*
*I have not mistreated people*
*I have not done evil instead of righteousness*
*I have not reviled the God*
*I have not laid violent hands on an orphan*
*I have not done what the God abominates*
*I have not killed*
*I have not turned anyone over to a killer*
*I have not caused anyone's suffering*
*I have not copulated (illicitly)*
*I have not been unchaste*
*I have not increased nor diminished the measure*
*I have not diminished the palm*
*I have not encroached upon the fields*
*I have not added to the balance weights*
*I have not tempered with the plumb bob of the balance*
*I have not taken milk from a child's mouth*

*I have not driven small cattle from their herbage*
*I have not stopped (the flow of) water in its seasons*
*I have not built a dam against flowing water*
*I have not quenched a fire in its time*
*I have not kept cattle away from the God's property*
*I have not blocked the God at his processions.'*

The weight of their heart was compared to that of a feather in one of the primary tests. This appears to be a test that would be failed by everyone. Egyptians believed that a person's heart would get heavier if he or she had committed sin during their lifetime. With ageing, the heart normally gains weight. It's possible that the Egyptians noticed this and concluded that the weight gain was due to sin. Unfortunately, it appears that the deceased individual will not be able to pass that test. The average adult heart weighs more than half a pound (227 grams). A male heart weighs between 280 and 340 grammes. The female heart weighs between 230 and 280 grammes. A feather is only a fraction of a pound in weight: *'The god Thoth would record the results and the monster Ammit would wait nearby to eat the heart should it prove unworthy.'* So the *Book of the Dead* says. Failure to pass this examination and to have one's heart eaten is probably not a good omen for one's future health. (illust. 25 & 26)

The feather of the goddess Ma'at, who represents order, truth, and justice, was used to weigh the heart of the deceased in the weighing of the heart rite. It was common practice to engrave 'Spell 30' on the heart scarabs of the departed. With this spell, you are telling your heart not to be a burden or a witness against the dead before that person who holds the balance of power. The heart scarab's construction is described in detail in a section of the spell: Myrrh was anointed on a scarab of nephrite adorned with gold before it was placed into the deceased person's chest, and the scarab's mouth was opened for him as a rite of passage.'

It was believed that the heart held the key to eternal life in Egyptian religion. For this reason, it was designed to be able to testify in the afterlife about its owner's character. The god Anubis would place your soul on one side of a giant set of scales and the feather on the other side. The soul was sometimes depicted as a tiny naked person. When the heart was weighed, it was supposed that Anubis and the gods would scrutinise it. If your soul weighed more than the feather of truth, you were unworthy, and Ammit the Devourer would eat your soul. (illust. 27)

Note: It's interesting that according to some historians, the *Ten Commandments* were derived from ancient Egyptian religion, and the Biblical Jews acquired the concept following their Exodus from Egypt. A list of things a man must swear to in order to enter the hereafter is found in Chapter 125 of the [Egyptian] *Book of the Dead* (a.k.a. the *Papyrus of Ani*). The substance and phrasing of these sworn utterances exhibit a striking resemblance to the *Ten Commandments*. There are further criteria in the *Book of the Dead*, which, of course, do not include Yahweh worship.

*The Book of the Dead* was written around 1800 BCE. The Hebrew Exodus from Egypt and the giving of the Ten Commandments on Mount Sinai, according to the *Schofield Reference Bible,* took place in 1491 BCE, three centuries later. Many religious liberals, historians, and secularists believe that the *Ten Commandments* in the Hebrew Scriptures were founded on this earlier writing, rather than the other way around.

# Death Rituals

**Compiled by Judith Page**

Ancient Egyptians used embalming and mummification in their funeral rites. The coffins in which the mummies were kept were embellished with images of the deceased. After that, the coffins were put in a stone sarcophagus for protection. It is true that the 'Opening of the Mouth' rite and other lesser known but no less significant Death Rituals were practiced. (illust.28)

Ritual was the most important aspect of Ancient Egyptian religion. It included the rituals of the priests, sacrifices, as well as magical incantations and enchantments. Both the living and the dead were thought to benefit from these rites. (illust. 29)

**Funeral Procession**
70 days after the death of a person, the embalmed body and casket were taken from the embalmer's tent, called an ibu, on the day of burial. The mummy was placed on a bier surrounded by protective statues of gods. When affluent Egyptians died, their funeral procession would have been an ostentatious display of luxury. Two female relatives or priestesses played the roles of the goddesses Isis and Nephthys and stood at either end of the coffin, which was generally pulled by oxen, the chief mourners in ancient Egyptian religion. A

jackal masked priest of the god Anubis was a key figure in these death rituals. Servants or slaves carrying the items that would be buried with the mummy in the tomb followed closely behind. Some participants were hired mourners, dancers, musicians, and priests, while others brought canopic jars and other burial goods. A sacrifice of freshly slaughtered calf's foreleg would be offered, along with poultry, meat, and vegetables.

**Funerary rites**
In front of the grave, the final burial rites were performed. The mummy was brought to its upright position. Priests carried out this complex rite to ensure that the departed could make full use of their senses in the afterlife. Purification, anointing, and recitation of prayers and spells were all part of this ritual, as was the use of ritual artifacts to restore the senses to the mummy. After that, the deceased was fed and clothed, and the mourners joined together in a burial feast. After that, the mummy was placed in the tomb's burial chamber, where it was given the final touches of preparation for its journey to the other side. (illust. 30)

**Opening of the Mouth Ceremony**
Traditional burial rites in Ancient Egypt were thought to reawaken the dead's senses, allowing them to partake of food and drink and speak in the afterlife. One of the most important Ancient Egyptian Death Rituals was The Opening of the Mouth ceremony's Death Rituals were as follows:

- An elaborate feast was served in honour of deceased loved ones who had begun their journey to the afterlife after all funeral procedures had been completed.
- These anthropoid coffins, or man-shaped, were commonly used in Ancient Egypt. Thus, the word anthropoid coffin is used to describe coffins shaped like human beings.
- The embalming priest with a jackal mask held the mummy in the standing position with its casket facing south. (illust. 31)

- A close member of the family burned incense.
- The women wailed loudly.
- The neck of the casket was decorated with garlands of flowers. The anthropomorphic coffin was painted with a likeness of the deceased.
- Another priest chanted potent spells.
- Death sacrifices were made of the food and drink, and the calf leg still spurting fresh blood.
- Ritual purification was conducted using salt and cow's milk.
- Death ceremonies known as Opening of the Mouth made use of embalming and coffin-making supplies. A priest used an adze to

touch the mouth, eyes, ears, and nose of the deceased so that they might accept the food offerings.
- After the Opening of the Mouth ceremonial and other death rituals were accomplished, the coffin and mummy were sealed in a sarcophagus.
- As the deceased began their journey into the afterlife, the ceremonies of the ancient Egyptians were marked with a feast and celebration. Any foods that had not been consumed were left for the scavenging dogs of the desert to eat.

## Wag Festival

This is one of the oldest festivals in ancient Egypt. As it was celebrated in the Old Kingdom, it would solely focus on the death and rebirth of the god Osiris, plus the souls of those who have passed and made their way to judgment and the afterlife. (illust. 32)

This festival followed the Wepet-Renpet in late August, but its date changed according to the lunar calendar. It was a tradition to create papyrus shrines and small papyrus boats that would sail across the Nile from the East bank to the West signifying the journey. People also honoured the dead by carrying food to their tombs and offering it to them. The celebration was led and performed by the priest belonging to the temple of Anubis. What does this remind you of?

## Rejuvenation and Rebirth

The Wag Festival was soon joined by the birth of the god Thoth and it became centred on rejuvenation and rebirth. Thoth was the god of writing, wisdom, and knowledge. He was associated with the judging of the dead by the God Osiris. This was the chain that linked both the gods. (illust. 33)

# Temples and the Priesthood

## Compiled by Judith Page

### Temple Organisation

The largest temple centres functioned as mini cities, employing a diverse range of people. It was a massive organisation, as evidenced by the fact that Karnak had over 81,000 employees! There were temple bakeries and breweries, and some temples possessed a fleet of boats and fishermen, as well as hunters and stables with donkeys, farms, and land tenants. The temple scribes recorded and maintained everything on sheets of papyrus as the produce arrived every day to fill the god's storehouses. In addition to the priests, the temple employed artisans such as stonemasons, painters, carpenters, weavers, scribes, and administrators.

### Wages

Any employee who worked in the temple was treated to a higher standard than usual. The god's wealth was to be shared by everybody, regardless of social standing or class of labour. Because large, well-functioning centres typically possessed extensive tracts of land, workers, stone masons, farmers, and others brought their families with them, increasing the population and ensuring that there were all kinds of supplementary demands and activities to keep women and children fed and clothed. Only the Royal House surpassed a huge religious temple complex in terms of wealth.

Ancient Egypt's priesthood has a long and illustrious history that is deeply steeped in tradition. Unlike the priesthoods common in Western society, the position of the Egyptian priest or priestess in society was significantly different. Rather than seeking the divine and developing a relationship with the gods, the priest's position was more analogous to that of a regular employee.

Due to the Pharaoh's inability to execute ceremonies at all of Egypt's temples, he selected high priests to perform the sacred rituals at each temple. Priestly roles were frequently passed down from father to son. In Egyptian society, priests had enormous power and money.

The priests' responsibilities included looking after the gods and attending to their needs. They also administered funeral rites, taught school, oversaw artists and works, and provided problem-solving advice.

Because the pharaoh was seen as a deity, the priests and priestesses were regarded as substitutes for him, as it was the priests' and priestesses' responsibility to keep Egyptian society in order. It was the most theoretically based of cultures. When one examines the elevated significance religion played in Egyptian culture, the mystical traits of the priests and priestesses take on secondary importance.

Religion served as a vehicle to control society, construct a hierarchy, and maintain the culture for future generations, as well as a way to meet the Egyptians' ethereal and basic wants. As a result, the priests' and priestesses' roles were on two levels, both utilitarian and magical.

In ancient Egypt, a priest or priestess was usually appointed by the monarch or gained a title passed down through the family. Priests who obtained their places by heredity or through the king were not exempt from everyday life in either circumstance. Indeed, such priests were expected to engage in everyday life to keep Egyptian civilisation running smoothly (and as stated above it was a position of high status). The priesthood began simply, with only a few temples, but as the dynasties progressed, the number of temples grew to hundreds. With such expansion, a massive bureaucracy was required to keep the temples in excellent repair. As a result, the Egyptian priesthood evolved from a few hundred priests to thousands, and with it, a priestly hierarchy.

The daily life of a priest or priestess depended on their sex and their hierarchical standing within the priesthood. Priests were often rotated from position to position within the priestly hierarchy and were integrated into and out of mundane society. This rotation system generally meant that a priest would enter into temple life for one month, three times a year. This rotation system had a direct connection to the often stringent purity rites of the priests.

There were several restrictions and traditions that a priest had to follow, regardless of his or her station. A priest or priestess could not eat fish (a food associated with peasant life), could not wear wool (as practically all animal products were considered unclean), was generally circumcised (only prevalent among male priests), and bathed three or four times a day in a sacred lake. It was also typical for oracle-tending priests (one of the most sacred roles) to shave off all their body hair, partly to get rid of lice, but also to purify themselves.

Stolists, or 'oracle' priests, were responsible for feeding and dressing the deity statues, as well as sealing the temple chambers at night. Because of the stolists' example, it is clear that the necessity for purity extended not just in this life, but also in the next. As a result of these purification rituals, priests were commonly referred to as the 'pure ones', regardless of their position in the temples.

In all temples, the process of appointing a new priest was essentially the same. All wickedness was washed away in a baptismal pool revered as a representation of Nu, the Cosmic Ocean. In order to be purified, the applicant was doused in oil and water before being taken to a statue of the Goddess and educated on how to work with it. After that, the applicant undertook a ten-day fast, during which time he or she had a spiritual or shamanic experience that unlocked the mysteries.

Classes of priests were established within the temple's structure. Large temples such as Karnak's administrators were a different group and one that was not so concerned with religious views. They oversaw the temple's finances and possessions. Different classes existed within the religious establishment as well. Each of the five priestly divisions in Amun's temple had its own subdivisions. All crafts were under the protection of Ptah; hence the High Priest at Men-nefer (Memphis) was referred to as 'the great chief of all artisans'. 'Prophets,' mistranslated from Egyptian as 'servants of the god', were largely royal appointments and could be chosen from any level of society. Ritual functions were carried out by them, leading the upper ranks of the priesthood.

Priests and priestesses performed both magical and economic duties in addition to their official roles in the Egyptian government. Nevertheless, lay magicians, who provided a commoner's perspective on Egyptian religion, were distinct from the priestly hierarchy. Lay magicians served their communities by offering counselling, magical arts, healing, and ceremonial services because of their faith in the gods and their connection to them.

The lay magicians who served in the Egyptian priesthood's final caste belonged to a vast temple known as 'The House of Life'. Laypeople would visit this place to have their dreams interpreted, to obtain magical spells and charms, to be healed, or to resist bad magic and obtain various forms of incantations. Despite the fact that the House of Life gave many prescribed remedies for common maladies to its laymen, it was shrouded in mystery in ancient times. In truth, the library of The House of Life was cloaked in secrecy since it contained numerous sacred rites, books, and temple secrets that were deemed to be harmful to the pharaoh, priests, and all of Egypt.

Though the magicians of The House of Life were considered a step down from the priests and their ceremonial duties, they were no less important, and as evidenced by the presence of many magical wands, papyri texts, and other archaeological evidence, The House of Life played a vital role in Ancient Egyptian culture.
The scribes were highly valued by both the pharaoh and the priesthood, to the point where the pharaoh himself is shown as a scribe in pictographs in some of the pharaoh's tombs. Scribes oversaw creating magical books, issuing royal decrees, keeping and recording burial ceremonies (particularly inside The Book of the Dead), and maintaining crucial records for Ancient Egypt's bureaucracy. Scribes spent years honing their talent of creating

hieroglyphics, and they merit special attention among the priestly caste because becoming a scribe in any Egyptian court or temple was considered the highest honour.

Finally, while there is a great deal of historical evidence indicating the role of priests within the priestly hierarchy, the rank of priestesses was at times equal, if not minor, to that of male priests. Within the temples of music and dancing, the female priestesses played the most important role. At Thebes, however, the chief priestess of Amun was known as the god's wife; she was the head of the god's harem of female musicians, who were affiliated with the goddess Hathor, the goddess of love and song. Such priestesses were effectively rulers of the theocracy during the Twenty-third Dynasty and afterwards, with their responsibilities centred on the veneration of Isis and numerous other female and male goddesses and gods.

The priestly hierarchy was made up of a variety of offices and responsibilities. The high-priest, also known as the Sem-priest and 'the First Prophet of the God', was at the top of the priestly order. Due to his age in years, the high-priest was often quite wise. He was not only the pharaoh's political advisor but also the political leader of the temples to which he belonged. The high priest was in charge of overseeing and counselling the pharaoh during magical rites and ceremonies. The high-priest held a ceremonial post and was frequently appointed as an advisor by the pharaoh; nonetheless, it was not rare for a high-priest to have risen through the ranks to his official status.

A number of priests served under the high priest, each with their own set of responsibilities. The second tier priests' specialisations ranged from 'horology' (keeping an accurate count of the hours through the days, which was extremely important during the time of the solar worshippers, but also for agricultural reasons), 'astrology' (which was extremely important to Egypt's mythology as well as its architectural and calendrical systems), and healing.
The cycles of the cosmos were immensely important, as seen by the priests' expertise, as they determined when crops would be sown, when the moon would wax or wane, and when the temple rites

would begin in the morning. The results of these Egyptian priests' research may be observed in both Egypt's mythical studies and agricultural techniques, which rival even the current Caesarean Calendar still in use today in the western world.

## The priesthood

Kher heb, or Lector Priest was required to read the sacred scrolls aloud from papyrus held open in his hands. Even if he had read them many times before, he was obliged to recite them exactly as written, as making a mistake could insult the god. When an image of the deity was carried out in front of the people, this was done at official events and at the head of processions.

The role of 'Hem netjer', or High Priest, did not include the responsibility to spread teachings about the god's superiority or to ensure the spiritual or moral welfare of the people. His duty was to tend to the god and the god's demands, acting as the god's servant. By honouring the god as an important Egyptian citizen, it was ensured that he would continue to care for his people. The highest priest was Pharaoh, who served as a servant to all the many gods at all the various religious centres around the land.

Depending on the size of the temple and the popularity of the cult, Pharaoh appointed a number of High Priests to act on his behalf at each temple. This appointment to High Priest was both religious and political and was sometimes passed down through generations of noble families.

## Hemet netjers ~ Female Servants of God

In the Old Kingdom, women from aristocratic households were accepted as 'hemet netjers'. Typically, they were associated with goddesses. It is unclear what work they performed beyond singing, dancing, and playing instruments. During the Third Intermediate Period, there was once a regal woman known as God's Wife of Amen. She was served by female acolytes, maintained chastity, and adopted a royal lady in order to ensure the succession.

## God's Father

The High Priest was also known as the First Prophet, and he had the authority to appoint delegates from the Second, Third, and Fourth Prophets. Aanen, Amenhotep III's brother-in-law, was for a long period the Second Prophet of Amen at Karnak and the High Priest of Ra-Atum. Yuya, Aanen's father, was the High Priest of Min at Akhim and also held the title of God's Father, which is thought to signify King's Father-in-law. However, 'father of the god' was also a title given to the priesthood below the First Prophet, and these individuals also had other important responsibilities outside of the temples. Yuya, in addition to being the High Priest of Min, was Master of the King's Horses and Overseer of the Cattle of the Min Temple.

**Temple Work and Purity**
The temple priesthood was divided into four groups, called phyles, and each of these phyles worked one month out of every three. Ritual purity was of the utmost importance in the temple. Each temple had its own sacred lake, where the priests cleansed themselves and the ritual utensils they used in rites, as well as where the water for the libation offerings was drawn. It was also part of the ritual/tradition that an ibis bird would first have to drink from the waters of the lake prior to any bathing. All animal products were deemed unclean; thus, priests could only wear white linen and papyrus sandals.

For the duration of his temple service, a priest removed all of his body hair, including his eyebrows, and would refrain from sexual activity. Outside of their temple responsibilities, they could marry, have children, and lead normal family lives.

**Services and Rituals**
The god was placed in a shrine, called a naos, which was built of stone or wood and kept in the temple's innermost chamber. The statue of the god might be constructed of stone, gold, or gilded wood, and it could be inlaid with semi-precious stones. It could be any size. It was not considered an idol, but rather a container for the deity's ka. At the shrine, ceremonies were performed three times a day, if not more. The Morning Hymn was sung by temple singers at dawn to awaken the god. After purifying himself, the priest leading the Morning Service broke the seal and untied the

bolts that had been secured the night before, allowing the god's doors to open. The god was now purified in a similar fashion to how the priests had been purified. In the same way that the King would have been dressed, perfumed, and cosmetics applied, incense was lit, so the god was also dressed, perfumed, and cosmetics applied.

## The Offerings

The god was then served food and drink. This was a showcase of the best that could be found: meat joints, roasted chicken, bread, fruits, vegetables, beer, wine, and everything else in enormous amounts, all from the temple's own kitchens, gardens and farms. Everything was of excellent quality. The meat came from animals that had been slaughtered out of sight of the god and inspected by a priest to ensure it was fit to be presented to the god. It was not permitted to display any abhorrent scenes before the god.

Other offerings would include garlands of flowers that would, in the case of larger temples, be grown in the temple gardens. Nothing was too great for the god.

The priest poured libations of water over the offerings, and incense was lit in a spoon-like saucer formed like a forearm with an open palm containing a small pot.. Incense was known as the 'Perfume of the Gods'. Employed to stimulate all the gods' senses, it was a significant part of the ceremonies. Taste was represented by food and drink, sound was represented by music and singing, and flowers were added to make the offering attractive and presentable. Thus, musicians, singers, and dancers entertained him while the god's ka was said to be absorbing these offerings. The hymns had a basic text with frequent repeats of the god's qualities and names, and the music could be sistrum or menat rattling, percussion, or, on rare occasions, harp, flute, drums, and cymbals.

## Festivals and Processions

Regular festival days, such as the First of the Month and the New Moon, were observed at the temples. The god's statue, placed on a bark, was then paraded around the temple grounds, with stops made for offerings at various points. The god's 'resting spots' were frequently associated with the festival.

Then there were the great religious celebrations, where the deity was transported to the perimeter of the temple courtyard to be viewed by the people. But the god was always hidden from the direct gaze of the commoner by a heavy veil. Ahead of the procession a priest would walk, carrying the sacred text on his shoulders.

Priests fanned and sheltered the god from the sun with ostrich plumes or fans made from palm leaves. At the rest stops along the road, incense was lit, and offerings were made. Some of these were temporary temples, while others were built just for the occasion. The bark was placed on an 'altar' while the ceremonies were carried out.

The bark was occasionally placed onto the god's own barge at the temple pier and hauled further down the Nile, escorted by a flotilla of boats. On occasions, the royal family was present to observe this. These were grand occasions to which everyone was invited, and they usually lasted several days, with plenty of food and drink.

Festivals, such as the remembrance of the Sacred Marriage of Hathor and Horus would be shared between two temples, Denderah and the Temple of Edfu. All these events had to take place at the correct time and on the correct day, and it was the temple astrologer's job to keep track of the religious calendars.

Such was the life of an ancient Egyptian priest.

# Dying Twice ~ Osiris

**Compiled by Judith Page**

The narrative of Plutarch thus comprises the following elements:
*The 'first death', inferred since Osiris is locked alive in the chest and then thrown into the water, from where the conclusion, commonly supposed, is that he had died by drowning.
*The first collection of Isis, as far as Byblos, in search of the body.
*The 'second death' of Osiris, cut in pieces by his brother Set. Pieces were once again thrown into the Nile.
*The second quest of Isis is in which she collects the pieces of her spouse's body and buries them separately or together, according to tradition (Isis and Osiris, 20-21).

The story of Osiris is nowhere to be found in a connected form in Egyptian literature, but everywhere, and in texts of all periods, the life, sufferings, death, and resurrection of Osiris are accepted as facts universally admitted. Greek writers have preserved in their works traditions concerning this god, and to Plutarch, we owe an important version of the legend as current in his day.

Few have bothered to look at Plutarch's account of this side of the death of Osiris, myself included. Perhaps with these two points of view, we can evaluate the myth with a more rational mind.

The comprehensive account that Plutarch provides, which focuses primarily on this aspect of the story of the murder of Osiris, deviates from the known Egyptian sources in several important areas. Plutarch, who used Greek names for many of the Egyptian deities, refers to Set as 'Typhon'. Plutarch also mentions a queen from ancient Ethiopia as one of the seventy-two individuals who conspire against Osiris (Nubia). Set commissions the creation of an exquisite chest that is tailored to Osiris's precise proportions.

Afterward, he makes the announcement during a banquet that he will give the chest as a present to whoever is able to fit inside it.

The visitors, in turn, lie inside the casket; however, nobody can fit within the coffin but Osiris. After Osiris has been placed into the chest his cohorts will immediately slam the lid down, place a seal around it, and then toss it into the Nile. The chest, which now contains the body of Osiris, is carried out to sea and eventually ends up in the city of Byblos, where a tree eventually grows around it.

The chest is still inside the tree when the king of Byblos chops it down to fashion it into a pillar for his palace. In order for Isis to recover the body of her husband, she must first remove the chest from its hiding place within the tree/pillar.

According to the legend Isis covered the pillar in fine linen, anointed it with oil, and returned it to the queen. Plutarch states that the piece of wood is still revered by the people of Byblos and kept in the temple of Isis. Prof. Robertson Smith argues (*Religion of the Semites,* p. 175) that the rite of draping and anointing a sacred stump provides the answer to the baffling question of the nature of the Ashera's ritual practices. 2 Kings xviii., 7.

This incident, which is not documented in Egyptian sources, provides an etiological account for the worship of Isis and Osiris that existed at Byblos during the time of Plutarch and probably as early as the New Kingdom. This cult is said to have originated in Byblos.

In another statement made by Plutarch, Set does not steal or dismember the corpse until after Isis has brought it back. Isis subsequently locates and entombs every component of her deceased husband's body, except for his male member, which she is forced to re-create via the use of magic as the original was consumed by fish in the river. This is the reason, according to Plutarch, why the Egyptians had a taboo against consuming fish in their culture.

However, in Egyptian sources, the penis of Osiris is found whole, and the only near comparison with this aspect of Plutarch's story is in a folk tale from the New Kingdom called 'The Tale of Two Brothers,' which has parallels to the Osiris myth.

The birth of Horus is the last point of contention in Plutarch's version of events. Before Osiris passed away, the form of Horus that exacts revenge on his father had already been conceived of and given birth to. Harpocrates, the second child to be born as a result of Osiris's posthumous union with Isis, is born prematurely and is not particularly healthy. In this part of Plutarch's retelling of the narrative, two of the numerous incarnations of Horus that can be found in Egyptian folklore are placed in roles that are distinct from one another.

Osiris controls Egypt, having inherited the throne from his forebears in a lineage that stretches back to the world's creator, Ra or Atum. His queen is Isis, one of the children of the earth god Geb and the sky goddess Nut, along with Osiris and his murderer, Set. There is little information regarding Osiris's rule in Egyptian sources; the emphasis is on his death and the events that follow. Osiris is associated with life-giving strength, just kingship, and the rule of Ma'at, the ideal natural order whose preservation was a primary goal in ancient Egyptian society. Set is synonymous with violence and disorder. As a result, the slaying of Osiris represents the conflict between order and chaos, as well as the interruption of existence caused by death.

According to a spell in the Pyramid Texts Osiris kicked Set in the face, but in a Late Period book, Set is upset because Osiris had sex with his consort Nephthys, the fourth child of Geb and Nut, who is Set's consort. The murder itself is repeatedly alluded to, but it is never explained in any detail. The writing of Osiris's death was avoided by the Egyptians because of their belief that written words had the power to change the world.

Even though most of the stories concerning Osiris make it quite apparent that he was killed, there were times when they flat-out denied that he had ever existed. In some of the interpretations of the texts, it is implied that Set kills Osiris by assuming the appearance of a wild animal, such as a crocodile or a bull. In other interpretations, it is said that Osiris's body is either thrown into the water or that he drowns. This later legend is the foundation of the Egyptian concept that persons who had perished in the Nile were sacred, and it was passed down from generation to generation. Even the identity of the victim can change, as it is sometimes the deity Harœris, an ancient form of Horus, who is killed by Set and subsequently avenged by another form of Horus, who is Harœris's son by Isis. However, in some versions of the story, Set is the one who is killed.

By the end of the New Kingdom, there was a legend that Set had dismembered Osiris and dispersed his body parts around Egypt. This story began during the New Kingdom. Osiris cult centres spread around the country, each made the claim that various parts of the body or the entire corpse were discovered close to their location. It is possible that the dismembered sections number as many as forty-two, with each fragment representing one of Egypt's Nomes (also known as provinces) in the country's current administrative structure. As a result, the god of kingship transforms into the personification of his kingdom. Isis, having taken the form of a bird, mates with Osiris, who has now passed away.

After Osiris's death, there is either a period in which Set succeeds to the throne or else there is no successor. During this time, Nephthys is assisting Isis in her search for the body of her husband. The two goddesses are often compared to falcons or kites when they are searching for or mourning Osiris. This may be because kites fly great distances in search of carrion, and the Egyptians associated their plaintive calls with cries of grief, or because of the goddesses' connection with Horus, who is often represented as a falcon.

With the aid of other deities including Anubis, God of embalming and funerary rites, and Thoth who too has great magical and healing powers, the goddesses Isis and Nephthys find and restore Osiris' body. He becomes the first to be mummified and the attempts of the gods to restore his body serve as the mythical basis for Egyptian embalming methods. These practices aimed to prevent the decomposition that occurs after a person dies. This portion of the narrative is frequently expanded with further episodes, in which Set or his henchmen attempt to cause harm to the body, and Isis and her companions' rally to protect it.

Isis becomes pregnant with Osiris' son and rightful heir, Horus, after Osiris has been healed. Isis, while remaining in her bird shape, is shown in other sources as fanning breath and life into Osiris's body while also copulating with him. This contrasts with the ambiguous spell that appears in the Coffin Texts and may indicate that Isis becomes pregnant because of a bolt of lightning.

However, the resurrection of Osiris does not appear to be permanent, and from this point forward in the narrative, he is only addressed as the ruler of the Duat, which is described as the realm of the dead in Ancient Egyptian mythology. Despite the fact that Osiris will only continue to exist in the Duat, both he and the monarchy that he represents will, in a sense, be reincarnated in his son, Horus. (illus. 34)

Isis guides the Boat of the Night as it passes through the Duat

# Rebirth and Initiation

**Compiled by Judith Page**

In the south-western corner of Karnak Temple, we locate a beautiful little temple complex known as the Opet, where the initiated would have learned the sacred secrecies. This location was a sanctuary of the Osirian Mysteries, and despite its size, is one of the most important places in all of Karnak. (illust. 35)

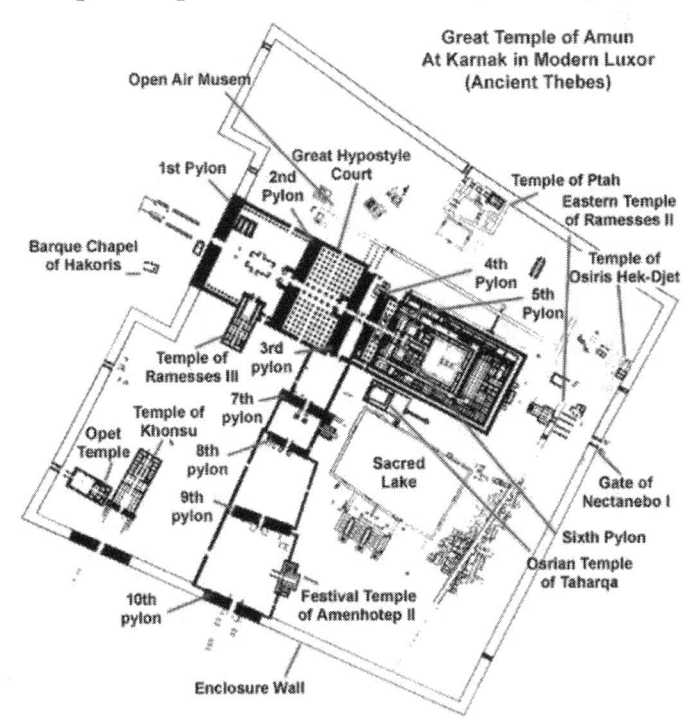

This modest but finely crafted sanctum is a veritable Tardis that provides a view into the inner life of an informed Pharaoh, as well as some insight into the significance of Egypt's famous yet exclusive Mysteries.

On the entrance jambs are carvings depicting the architect Ptolemy being led into the presence of holy Osiris himself. One enters an oblong portico above which is a colourful and heavily engraved roof supported by two magnificent reeded and flowered columns, each of which was surmounted with Hathor's staring visage. Two small windows with stone gratings are in the east wall, allowing weak light to creep through. (illust. 36)

A little vestibule beyond this has walls adorned in bold bas-reliefs and vertical lines of hieroglyphs. And, in contrast to the ruins of most other temples still remaining, three well intact entrances lead out of the vestibule's end and side walls. Each lintel is crowned by an architrave of more than twenty magnificent cobras. The serpents are not just half-reliefs chiselled into the surface of the wall, but full sculptures with raised heads and extending hoods. The classic winged sun insignia hangs on a ledge beneath each line, making a magnificent decoration almost one yard high (one metre).

The royal cobra adornments indicate that the three chambers to which the doors provided access were important in the temple plan. As you proceed through the doorway at the far end (the doors themselves no longer exist, but the top and bottom holes into which the posts were put are clearly visible) you come to a little shrine whose sides represented the monarch in adoration and the goddess Hathor's banner. A large break in the stone flooring yawns beneath it, revealing the shattered entrance to a subterranean tomb. Going back into the two side-chambers there are two holes in the corners that led to the same crypt and an underground corridor. Indeed, the entire area is honeycombed with subterranean vaults and corridors; to the right of the portico, two more floor-gaps open above small hallways.

What did these mysterious crypts and corridors mean? They can be likened to the subterranean complex of rooms found in the moat-bordered crypt in Abydos, dug forty feet (12.192m) below the surface of the ground level. One can indeed wonder about the tomb-like setting that is a reminder of the re-enactment of the ancient rite that dramatised Osiris' death and resurrection—that rite carved in stone on the walls of the small Mystery Temple on Denderah's roof-terrace.

Why were these dismal, dark places chosen for these mysterious initiations?
Three reasons are given:
- to ensure complete safety and secrecy for a privileged and dangerous experiment;
- facilitate the candidate's entrance by obscuring his surroundings and thus preventing distraction from the interior state;
- and to ensure the candidate's easier entrance by obscuring his surroundings.

For initiates, the ritual experience of being admitted into these cults took them bodily into the underworld, so that afterward their conviction about the possibility of an afterlife became unshakable, and the rest of their life was devoted to pursuing immortality and godhood in the afterlife.

In the words of Plutarch, '... the initiate, perfect by now, set free and loose from all bondage, walks about, crowned with a wreath, celebrating the festival together with the other pure people, and he looks down on the uninitiated, unpurified crowd in this world in mud and fog beneath his feet.'

A perfect ancient symbolism of spiritual darkness and ignorance, which the hierophants found their candidate in at the beginning of his initiation, is provided by the fact that upon awakening, he would open his eyes to the sun's rays in another place, where he would be carried toward the end of this spiritual illumination experience. After a lengthy initiation that began at night and finished with the break of day, the newly made initiate had emerged from materialistic ignorance into spiritual insight (light).

The Mysteries' secret ceremonies were only performed in underground crypts, reserved chambers near the holy shrine, or small temples built on the rooftops; they were never performed anywhere else. All these locations were off-limits to the public, who were warned not to approach them under any circumstances.

The hierophants who agreed to initiate a candidate took on a great deal of responsibility. It was up to them whether he lived or died. An unforeseen invader interrupting a sacred process of initiation resulted in his death, much as an unexpected incursion into a delicate surgical operation may result in the unfortunate patient's death in our time. After all, what was initiation if not a form of psychic surgery, a separation of the spiritual and corporeal aspects of man?

As a result, initiatory chambers were hidden and heavily guarded. Those chambers which lay near a great temple's shrine would have to be approached in total darkness. The light faded as one exited the doorway, eventually disappearing entirely when the sacred shrine's threshold was reached. The candidate's body was left in this safe darkness until the moment of his initiation, at which point he was brought out into the light.

Those chambers that were underground vaults epitomised the crypts that were both symbolic and literal tombs. The candidate was guided to this stage by Anubis, the jackal-headed god, and Master of the Mysteries. According to the ancient papyri, it is Anubis who leads one past the threshold of the unseen realm, into the presence of horrific apparitions.

The knowledge imparted in these schools of initiation was transmitted directly from the earliest revelation of the truth to the earliest civilisations and had to be guarded to preserve its integrity. One may therefore comprehend why these secrets were carefully concealed from the common populace.

The state in which the initiate-candidate found himself must not be mistaken for ordinary slumber. It was a magical sleep in which he stayed paradoxically awake but, to another world.

Also, it would be a mistake to think that such an exalted experience was the work of a modern hypnotist. The latter throws his subject into a strange situation that neither of them fully understands. On the other hand, the hierophant of the Mysteries had secret traditional knowledge that gave him the ability to use his power as if he knew everything. The hypnotist taps into the subconscious mind of his hypnotised subject down to a certain level, but he doesn't experience the change himself. The hierophant, on the other hand, used his own perceptive powers to watch and control every change. Above all, the hypnotist can only get his subject to talk about things that have to do with our physical world and life or to do strange things with their physical bodies. The hierophant went further and could guide the candidate's mind step by step through an experience that involved the spiritual world. This is something that no modern hypnotist could do.

The intriguing drama of Osiris' innermost secret rite is evidenced by wall engravings in temples. That august rite was nothing more than a process that combined hypnotic, magical, and spiritual forces to free the candidate's soul from the heavy bonds of his fleshly body for a few hours, and sometimes for a few days, so that he could live with the memory of this epoch-making experience and conduct himself accordingly for the rest of his life. He was now able to accept the survival of the soul after death, which was accepted by most men through trust in their religion. He was fortified in his conviction by personal knowledge.

Who were these hierophants, whose power could cause such a miraculous metamorphosis in a man? These venerable stewards of higher learning were, by definition, few in number. They once embraced all of Egypt's High Priests, as well as select senior members of the priesthood. Their knowledge was guarded with utmost secrecy and kept so exclusive that Egypt's name became synonymous with mystery in classical times.

In the Egyptian halls of the Louvre Museum in Paris, there is a tomb of Ptah-Mer, High Priest of Memphis, which carries an epitaph with the words: 'He delved into the Mysteries of every sanctuary, uncovering nothing. He hid everything he had seen behind a veil.' The hierophants were forced to maintain this exceptional reserve for their own reasons, but the necessity of removing the sceptic and scoffer from operations involving so much danger to the candidate's life is evident, as is the inadvisability of casting pearls before swine. However, it was more than possible that most men were not properly ready or prepared to embark on such an experience, which could easily lead to madness or death, and thus it was restricted to a select few.

Many people knocked on the doors of the Mystery Temples in vain, while those who applied were subjected to a series of examinations that either broke their nerve or decreased their desire for initiation.

The Mysteries became the most exclusive institution of antique times through a process of elimination — and exclusive selection — and the secrets revealed beyond their well-guarded doors were always transmitted under solemn pledge that they would never be divulged. Every man who passed through those doors became a member of a secret society that moved and worked with more purpose and wisdom amid the profane multitude. *'Those who have engaged in the Mysteries are supposed to become more spiritual, more just, and better in every manner,'* wrote Diodorus.

These initiations were not unique to Egypt; ancient civilisations inherited these Mysteries from antiquity, and they were part of a fundamental revelation from the gods to the human race. Almost every pre-Christian people had their own institution and tradition of the Mysteries. The Romans, Celts, British Druids, Greeks, Cretans, Syrians, Hindus, Persians, Mayas, and American Indians, among others, had analogous temples and rites with a system of graduated illuminations for initiates. Aristotle did not hesitate to declare that the Eleusinian Mysteries safeguarded Greece's welfare. Socrates observed that *'those who are acquainted with the Mysteries insure to themselves very pleasing hopes against the hour of death'.* Sophocles the playwright, Menippus of Babylon, Aristides the orator, Eschylus the poet, Solon the law-giver, Cicero, Herodotus of Ephesus, Pindar, and Pythagoras are among the ancients who have confessed or hinted that they had been initiated.

Even today, the trainee is taken through a course of the spiritual Mysteries in the advanced degrees of the discipline of Ju-jitsu in Japan; degrees which are known only to a rare few since they deal with secrets that are appropriate only for a few. The trainee is forced to participate in an initiation ceremony in which he is strangled by a master. The actual strangulation takes only a minute to complete, after which the applicant collapses onto a couch, effectively dead.

During this condition, his spirit is released from his body and has an experience of worlds beyond our own. When the stipulated period of death has passed, his master resurrects him using a strange method known only as 'kwappo'. He who emerges from this wonderful experience is an initiate. Even now, Freemasonry carries a vestige and relic of ancient institutions; its origins can be traced to ancient Egypt. Do Craft members recall that Pythagoras was initiated in Egypt? Some of the important symbols of the Egyptian Mysteries were taken by those who created the degrees of Masonry.

The inevitable degeneration of mankind resulted in the disappearance or withdrawal of true hierophants and their replacement by unillumined men, resulting in the degradation of the Mysteries into baneful caricatures of their former selves. The evilness of man sought the powers of black magic, and eventually conquered these institutions in Egypt and elsewhere. That which was once sacred, exclusive, and devoted to keeping a flame of spiritual knowledge, pure occult knowledge, and pure occult knowledge, pure – has gone.

Even if their secrets have perished with them, the distinguished list of names of men who sought and discovered, or were offered and accepted, the exquisite experience of such initiation in their earlier days attests to the knowledge they conferred on men.

Many papyrus texts and wall inscriptions demonstrate how deeply the early Egyptians adored the Osirian ceremony, and how the masses regarded those who were allowed to enter the secluded shrines and dedicated crypts where the most sacred and innermost aspects of the rite were performed, with awe. For there was an exalted and last degree of initiation when men's souls were transported up to the highest spheres of being, to the realm of the Creator Himself, not just temporarily emancipated from their bodies in a state of simulated death, but to illustrate the truth of survival after the great transition.

The finite mind of man was dragged into contact with the limitless mind of his superior divinity during this wonderful encounter. He was able to come into silent, spell-bound communication for a brief moment, with the Father of All. And this small moment of exquisite joy was enough to change his entire outlook on life. He'd consumed the most sacred food on the planet. He'd found the ineffable ray of Deity that was his true innermost self, of which the soul-body that transcends death was only the intangible vesture. In truth and fact, he was reborn in the highest sense. He who had been initiated in this way became a perfect Adept, and the hieroglyphic inscriptions describe him as someone who may expect the gods' favour throughout his lifetime and a state of paradise after death.

Although superficially like the hypnotic entrancements of the earlier degrees of initiation, such an experience came with an augmentation that was inwardly radically distinct. It could never be bestowed by hypnotic power or invoked by a magical ceremony.

Only the supreme hierophants, who are one with their divinities and whose wills mix with his, might stir the candidate to realisation of his greater nature by their incredible divine force. This was the noblest and most astounding discovery available to an Egyptian man at the time, and it is still available to modern man, albeit in different ways.

The initiation experience was a miniature version of the experience that would eventually be shared by the entire human race as a result of evolutionary processes; the only difference being that, because the former was a forced, accelerated growth, an artificial process such as enhancement was used, whereas with the latter, both psychic and spiritual development would occur naturally.

As a result, the experience reimagined the entire drama of human evolution, as well as humanity's inevitable doom, within the soul. The underlying premise was that a man's normal worldly nature might be momentarily paralysed by a deep sluggish sleep, and his normally unnoticed psychic or spiritual nature could be awakened by procedures only known to the hierophant. A man who was artificially put into such a coma would appear to an onlooker to be physically dead; in actuality, he would be said to have 'descended into the tomb' or 'buried in the tomb' in the symbolical language of the Mysteries.

The candidate would be truly dead to all earthly things, while his consciousness, his soul-being, would briefly separate itself from the flesh, having been bereft of his corporeal energy and having the force of his personal passions and desires temporarily soothed. Only in this state could a man view the spirit world as it was perceived by the spirits themselves, witness visions of gods and angels, travel across boundless space, learn about his deepest self, and, eventually, learn about the true God.

Such a man could legitimately claim to have been both dead and raised, to have slept in the tomb and passed through the miracle of resuscitation, rising to discover a fresh comprehension of the importance of death and to live a more spiritual life. The imprint of his hierophant, who had brought all of this about, was on him, and the two would be invisibly linked by the closest, deepest tie for the rest of their lives. The notion of the immortality of the soul was no longer just a theory; it was a proven fact that had been thoroughly proven to him.

When the initiate awoke to the light of day, he could validly state that he had returned to the world entirely transformed and spiritually reborn. He had been to hell and heaven and knew some of their mysteries. If he promised to keep those secrets safe, he also promised to live and behave himself in the future based on those worlds' true existence. He went among men with total certainty of immortality, and while he kept the origins of that certainty to himself, he couldn't help but communicate some faith in that certainty to his fellow beings, even if unknowingly. By the strange subconscious telepathy that always travels between men, he revived their hopes and confirmed their trust.

His belief in death had faded; instead, he believed in endless, self-existent, and conscious Life; he no longer believed in the concept of death. He was convinced that the soul existed and that it was a ray from the central sun, God, for him when his hierophant revealed this to him in the temple's guarded recesses. As time passed, the myth of Osiris took on a deeper significance for him. He also discovered Osiris, who was already a part of him and had been reincarnated.

However, Egypt's earliest holy literature, The Book of the Dead, is a mixture of papyri relating to the dead and the presumably dead — the initiated — and is thus rather confused. This was the genuine teaching of Egypt's oldest sacred text. According to the phrase, 'This is a book of exceeding great mystery', the Mysteries had it in its original, unaltered form. Let no man see it, for that would be an abomination. Conceal its existence. Its title is 'The Book of the Master of the Secret Temple'.

Therefore, he prefixed his own name in The Book of the Dead with 'Osiris', which is a reference to the god Osiris. 'I am Osiris,' the deceased states in the earliest versions of the ancient book. Thus, the current view of Osiris as the seemingly dead entombed initiate is supported.

In the papyrus of Nu, the ecstatic initiation declares much more emphatically: *'I, even I, am Osiris. I have become glorious. I have sat in the birth chamber of Osiris, and I was born with him, and I renew my youth along with him. I have opened the mouth of the gods. I sit upon the place where he sitteth'.*

And, in other papyri of this ancient Book: 'I raise myself to venerated God, the Master of the Great House'.

That's what students were taught in the Mysteries, a revered institution in antiquity that's mostly ignored today.

This means that we can have a better sense of the true meaning of ancient religious practices when we realise that their heroes represent the human spirit, and their exploits represent their journey to heaven. As a result, according to the ancient Egyptians, Osiris becomes a symbol of the divine element in man, as well as a symbol of that element's descent into the material world and return to spiritual consciousness.

His reputed fragmentation into fourteen or forty-two parts represented the human being's current spiritual dissection into a creature whose once-perfect harmony has been shattered. His reason has been torn from his feelings, his flesh from his spirit, and he is torn between confusion and cross-purposes. Similarly, the story of Isis gathering the fragments of Osiris' body and bringing them back to life symbolised the restoration — in the Mysteries at the time, and later by evolution — of man's warring nature to perfect harmony: the kind of harmony in which spirit and body work in unison, and reason follows the path of feeling. It was the re-establishment of fundamental unity.

The Egyptians' ultimate belief, which served as the theoretical foundation for the highest degrees of initiation, was that man's soul must finally return to the divine Being from which it was first rayed out, a process they called 'becoming Osiris'. Even here on Earth, they considered *man* to be an Osiris.

The candidate's liberated soul is directed to protect itself in its long and deadly journeys through the underworld not only by using amulets, but by openly announcing, 'I am Osiris', according to their secret initiation manual, the Book of the Dead. *'O blind soul I Arm thyself with the torch of the Mysteries and in the earthly night, thou shalt discover thy luminous Double, thy celestial Self. Follow this divine guide and he will be thy Genius. For he holds the key to thy existence, past and future,'* says the same sacred Scripture.

Initiation, then, meant entering into a new way of life, a spiritual way of existence that the human race had lost when it fell from 'paradise' into 'matter' in the distant past. The Mysteries were a method of inward re-ascension, leading to a perfect condition of illumination grade by grade. They first revealed the worlds beyond the realm of physical matter, and then they revealed the greatest mystery of all—man's own divinity.

They revealed infernal worlds to the candidate to test his character and tenacity, as well as to instruct him, and heavenly worlds to encourage and bless him. Just because they used the entrance-ment method doesn't mean no alternative option existed or exists. It was their way, but there are other ways to find the kingdom, including ways without trance.

Who among us can match the wonderful words of the Roman philosopher-initiate, who said: 'Where we are, death is not; where death is, we are not. It is the last, best boon of nature; for it frees man from all his cares. It is, at the worst, the close of a banquet we have enjoyed.'

Our perspective on death gives a crucial indicator of our outlook on life. The Mysteries impacted a man's perspective on death and, consequently, his behaviour in life. They demonstrated that Death is merely the flip side of the Life coin.

Once dismissed as whimsical nonsense, the scientific, psychical, and psychological study is now altering the Western world's perspective on once dismissed topics. Modern research is rescuing ancient concepts from the unwarranted disdain in which they have languished while newer ideas have matured. We are beginning to see sanity in the apparent lunacy of ancient civilisations. In many respects, we are coming to see and appreciate that their understanding of the capabilities and qualities of the human mind was far superior to ours. Our agnostic age has been surprised by the emergence of immaterial forces.

Our most distinguished scientists and philosophers are joining the ranks of those who believe that life has a psychological component. What they believe today, the majority will believe tomorrow. We began, possibly appropriately, as full sceptics; by the conclusion, we will be complete believers. An interesting thought. We will rescue belief in the soul from the chill of contemporary scepticism. The first great message of the ancient Mysteries—'There is no death?'—will be disseminated to the whole world, despite the fact that only a select few will be able to personally verify its veracity. I have to say, that at this moment in time, I believe in nothing, I either 'know', or I 'doubt' something to be true.

The concept of survival does not necessarily entail that we will all emerge from our coffins in the distant future. To meld ourselves with the physical dwellings in which we reside is hardly indicative of our intelligence. Both in the medieval European and the uninitiated Egyptian mind, the word resurrection has acquired a false, simply material sense, therefore we must learn the principles that regulate the secret constitution of man. The greatest minds of antiquity, the initiates of the Mysteries, were au fait with these laws; nevertheless, whilst their lips were sealed and their truths were concealed in the gloom of temple crypts, no such restriction is imposed on us now. I like to look at the image of a sculpture dated to ca. 2455-2350 BCE of a young Egyptian boy named Ankhmara with his finger on his lips.

A day arose, in the decline and fall of Egypt, as in the decline and fall of all other ancient nations, when the prophecy of Egypt's own early Prophet Hermes literally came to pass: 'O Egypt, Egypt! the land which was the seat of divinity shall be deprived of the presence of the gods. There shall not remain more of thy religion than tales, than words inscribed on stone and telling of thy lost piety. A day will come, alas, when the sacred hieroglyphs will become but idols. The world will mistake the symbols of wisdom for gods and accuse great Egypt of having worshipped hell-monsters'.

Such were the Mysteries!

The most magnificent institutions of the ancient world…have disappeared. Control of the Mysteries eventually fell into the wrong hands; into the hands of unscrupulous, selfish men eager to exploit the power of this tremendous institution—before whom proud Pharaohs occasionally bowed—all for their own personal gain. Many priests became focal points for potent evil, practising the heinous rites and dark incantations of black magic; some were High Priests—supposed to be the gods' ministers to man—became devils in human form, summoning the most heinous demons from the underworld for the most odious of reasons. In high places, sorcery took the place of spirituality.

The Mysteries soon lost their genuine nature and exalted purpose during the spiritual gloom and disorder that descended upon the kingdom, and worthy candidates were difficult to find—fewer and fewer in number as time passed. The qualified hierophants began to die out swiftly, as if by some mysterious Nemesis, and all but ceased to exist as a body. They died without leaving enough heirs to carry on the family line. They were replaced by unworthy men. The few who remained, unable to fully fulfill their allocated part in the world, met their fate. They closed their hidden writings, left their underground crypts and temple chambers, took one last regretful glance at the ancient abodes, and departed, sadly but peacefully.

They had seen Nature's inevitable preparation for a reaction far away on the horizon of Egypt's destiny. They'd seen a wisp of light that was preordained to pierce their country's sky and spread. They had seen the Christ's star—he who would reveal the fundamental truth of the Mystery teaching to the entire world, without restraint or secrecy. As one of Christ's Apostles declared, 'the Mystery which has been hidden from ages and generations' will be revealed to the unprivileged masses and common folk. Via the simple force of faith, what the archaic institutions transmitted to a select few through a rigorous procedure would be communicated to all people. Yeshua, or Jesus had far too much love in his heart to provide for a select few; he desired to save the masses. He showed them a path that required nothing more than faith in his words; he did not offer them any hidden esoteric initiation process. It was, however, a path that could provide those who accepted it with the same certainty of immortality as the Mysteries.

The Open Path according to Jesus, taught humility and asked for help from a higher power, a power that was always ready to give complete certainty just by being in the hearts of those who let it in. Jesus only asked that people follow his teachings and be humble enough to stop taking credit for their own ideas. In return, he offered the greatest reward of all: the awareness of the Father. He knew that in that presence, all doubts would disappear, and man would understand the truth of immortality without having to be hypnotised. Man would know this because the Father's Mind would have filled his own mind, and this indescribable filling would turn simple faith into divine intuition. This was not a form of belief, but control and indoctrination of the masses.

So were dosed for the last time, the doors of Egyptian Mystery Schools, and no hopeful candidates' feet passed up the hallowed step that led towards the temple entrance, or down the darkening sloping tunnel to the temple crypt.

But, as history shows, what has been, will be again; gloom and confusion have returned, and man's instinctive need to re-establish communication with the higher worlds has troubled him once more. As a result, it is the writer's goal that conditions, circumstances, and the right people will be found to replant a modern version of those Mysteries in each of our world's five continents, completely adapted to suit our changing age.

# What is Heka ~ Magic

### by Judith Page

In ancient Egypt there was no religion, the ancients practiced magic. To define this: religion is, or should be, focused upon offering veneration to the divine, the focus is thus divine, not humanity. Magic, however, is concerned with manipulating the divine for our own ends. It is focused upon and devised for human beings; the divine is simply a tool for the realisation of human needs and wants. Religion is theocentric; magic is anthropocentric. The ancient Egyptian word for magic is Heka or Hekau.

In the 1920s when the tomb of the boy-king Tutankhamen was opened, folk were swayed by Tut-mania, as opposed to the category of Egyptophilia 'lovers of things Egyptian'.

So many visitors to Egypt, and indeed to the museums of the world displaying the great works, will experience the visual and written art of an era that universally resonates with our wonderment of things enigmatic and arcane. And at times this seems to overdo the visual or aesthetic value of the artifacts and obscures the profound meaning of pharaonic Egypt's metaphysical legacy.

It is this mysterious quest that initially attracts many to the study of Egypt, and further toward its religious and philosophical tenets, then ultimately to its sacred science—a subject some in the modern world mistakenly refer to as 'magic'.

The nineteenth-century mathematician, mystic, and scholar, Rene Adolphe Schwaller de Lubicz, popularised the idea of sacred science in ancient Egypt during his study of art and architecture of the Temple of Luxor and his subsequent book, *The Temple of Man*. The ancient Egyptians viewed magic – that imperceptible power that changes visible reality – as an essential and potentially active function that exists in every living being. This function, called Heka, was the first feature radiated by the Sun-god Ra when he declared that he would create the universe. At that moment, Heka came into being, as both an extension of Ra and as a separate entity. From this event, the creation proceeded, and thus everything that followed possessed a degree of Heka.

In an Old Kingdom (BCE 2700-2180) royal text, this power was cited as an endowment to the human race:
*'He made heka for them, to use as a weapon for warding off occurrences. And he made them dreams for the night, to see the things of the day.'* — Instruction for King Merikare, 10th Dynasty

At that time, there was no difference between 'good' and 'bad' magical power, or whether it represented the qualities of 'black' or 'white'. In the polytheistic universe of ancient Egypt, such dualities were easily resolved by divine beings and forces that possessed both constructive and destructive aspects. It was the mere intent alone that determined the differences in their effects, and this could include protection, an intent to please, approval or hatred, or devotion.

The key to activating this power, Heka lay primarily in the use of *Iru* (creating a ritual act) and uttering *Medu Neter*, 'divine words'. It was believed that magical spells and visualisations were given to the human race by the gods themselves – the celestial magician Djehuty, or Thoth who brought forth the word of creation, and the artisan of the universe Ptah, who generated the power to manufacture and infuse objects with life.

From their traditions of magical actions among gods and mortals that took place in timeless time, in other words, the effects of real-time, communication were instantaneous. In those days mortals were much closer to the Gods, and the ancient Egyptians understood that the world of possibilities, transcending life and death, was accessible to one in possession of the words and acts of creation. Heka, 'words of power'.

This true story confirms the rationalist's error in supposing that the unexpected, the evidently unfounded, appears as magic to the simple mind. The latter may be terrified by the phenomenon but will always search for its cause.

The law of causality is not missing from the magical phenomenon. *Between cause and effect, there exists a bond, and that bond is called Neter.* It is this *Neter* that the believer hopes to spur into action through his appeal. Furthermore, what this *Neter* represents as energetic and harmonic activity is consciously evoked by the sage. This conscious evocation must essentially be a gesture or a word of the same nature as that of the *Neter* they have summoned, and by that statement, *the evocation becomes the cause of the magical effect.*

Even the ancient Egyptians realised that only the Creator can make something out of nothing. The connecting link between cause and effect is mysterious only for the ignoramus who thinks of the *Neter* in the form of a human being.

Names too were equally as powerful as words and acts in Egyptian magic, and the possession of names gives power over the named, and at the same time reveals the powers of the named.
Preservation of the parts of a being caused the deceased to remember his name after death. The name was regarded as a vital part of being. It begins:
*'I have put my name in the Upper Egyptian shrine. I [have] made my name to be remembered in the Lower Egyptian shrine, on this night of the counting of years and numbering of months'.* – Book of the Dead, spell 25.

In this way, possessing divine names at birth, initiation, and inauguration, granted powers that could bring one the protection and counselling of divine beings.

By the Middle Kingdom, five names or divine roles in total were ascribed to monarchs, each designating a sacred function that was overseen by the gods. In the tomb of Tutankhamen, for example, the name of the king in his role as Horus is given as:

- *Heru: Ka Nakht, Tut Mesut* ('Horus: Strong bull, of perfect birth'). In addition to his Horus name, the young king was known as
- *Nebty: Nefer Hepu Segereh Taui* ('He of the Good Laws, Who Pacifies the Two Lands'). This name was under the guardianship of Nekhebet and Wadjet, the two goddesses of Upper and Lower Egypt, respectively. Tutankhamen also possessed a Golden Horus name, one that identified his kinship to the gods, as their son on earth. In this role, he was known as
- *Heru Nebu: Wetches Khau Sehotep Neteru* ('He who Wears the Crowns and Satisfies the Gods'). As ruler of the two regions of Egypt, he also possessed a throne name, the
- *Nesu Bity* ('King of Upper and Lower Egypt') and this is Nebkheperura ('all the transformations of Ra'). And lastly, we know him by his birth name, the
- *Sa Ra* ('Son of the Sun'), Tutankhamen ('the living image of Amen').

In the light of this, the 'name' is received when initiated, and this name is known only to the Neters, the Gods.

# The Anubieion ~ A Dark Time

**Compiled by Judith Page**

*'Who has not heard, Volusius, of the monstrous deities those crazy Egyptians worship? One lot adores crocodiles, another worships the snake-gorged ibis...you'll find whole cities devoted to cats, or to river-fish or dogs...'* Juvenal wrote his Satire XV around CE 128-130[1]

### The Dog Catacombs

During the 19th century Jacques Jean Marie de Morgan, geologist and archaeologist, was the director of antiquities in Egypt. He excavated in Memphis and Dashur, creating countless drawings of many Egyptian pyramids. In 1897 he published his Carte de la Nécropole Memphite (Map of the Memphite Necropolis) on which two catacombs marked 'Tombes des chiens (A) and (B)' appear. The key to the map dates them to the New Kingdom (1550-1069 BCE). (illust. 37)

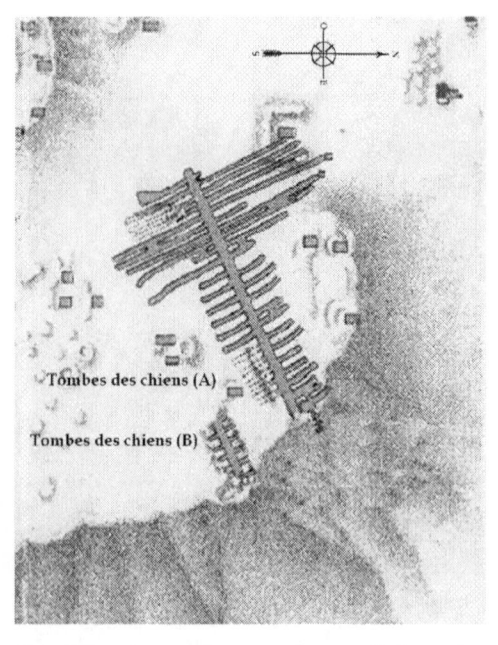

Although two catacombs are depicted on De Morgan's map from 1897, the smaller one (B) is currently inaccessible due to significant sand drifting. It's possible that some of it fell during the 1992 earthquake, when a sizable hole suddenly developed just to the north of the Emery house, roughly where the (B) catacomb was situated. In spite of this, it is known that this catacomb shared the same shape as its much larger neighbour (A) to the north, consisting of an axial corridor that ran roughly east-west and a number of galleries that opened from it to the north and south.

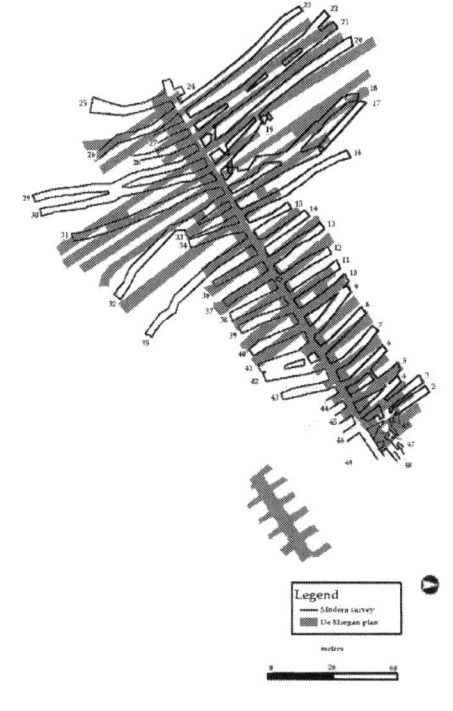

The De Morgan plan specifies a maximum width of 82 feet (25 metres) for the complex and a length of roughly 148 feet (45 metres) for the axis. The length of each gallery ranges from 23 to 33 feet (7 to 10 metres). Most of the burials took place in these tunnels or galleries. (illust. 38)

The discoverer of these dog-mummified catacombs is unknown, only that they came to light on a map of the Saqqara necropolis by Jacques de Morgan. The plan is on a very small scale and gives very little detail and is located just a few yards from the future site of Professor Emery's dig home. The only information De Morgan provides about the catacombs is a hint in his colour key that they might be from the New Kingdom.

Bubastieion and Anubieion, a Late Period temple-town, are located in Saqqara. Two enormous neighbouring brick precincts, the Anubieion (Temple of Anubis) in the north and the Bubasteion (Temple of Bastet) in the south, are located at the desert escarpment along the north-eastern edge of the Saqqara cemetery, next to the pyramid of Teti. Although little remains of these buildings, it is believed that they date to King Ahmose's reign (570-526 BCE – 26th Dynasty). King Nakhtnebef (Nectanebos I,380–362 BCE) of the 30th Dynasty extended the enclosures and also constructed other temples. Only a handful of the temples' foundation walls have survived, even though they were all built on terraces. The monuments' initial placements and orientations are therefore still vague.

**Animal Cults**
Even though there was only ever one living Apis bull, and it was buried with royal honours, the majority of animal cults were an aspect of 'popular' belief. Most of the ibises, falcons, cats, and dogs are believed to have been sacrificed as offerings to Saqqara by what is most appropriately thought of as 'pilgrims'. The mummies may have been presented as a token of gratitude for some success attributed to the god.

The ancient Egyptians were obsessed with death and everything they did to prepare for mummification was really looking at life after death as a way of perpetuating oneself forever.

An animal would be killed for you by the priests, mummified, and then interred in a catacomb in your honour. This was a means of gaining favour with whatever god you were a devotee of.

It's believed that travellers may have approached temple priests if they wanted to leave votives or tribute mummies. It is entirely possible that pilgrims who visited the Anubieion Temple would have seen healthy adult dogs kept there and believed that a payment made for the burial of one of the god's representatives would secure the burial of one of these animals in due course instead of the funds being used for a representative neonate burial, according to the study.

It's also conceivable that pilgrims brought a newborn mummy to Saqqara having acquired it from a nearby farm, and that this was perfectly appropriate regardless of the animal's age because the goal of the ritual was to obtain a respectable burial for the god's representative. The animal cults are difficult to comprehend within the context of twenty-first-century notions because the individual creature's existence may have been relatively brief but its journey to the hereafter was to be a good one, and the afterlife was eternal.

After being separated from their mothers, these young animals must have either been intentionally slaughtered or permitted to die before being mummified. However, it is important to bear in mind that the Egyptians would not have viewed this as cruel. The devotees intended to conduct a good deed for a symbol of Anubis by giving the animal a burial befitting a god that would last forever. We suppose that mass graves for dogs occurred once a year, as is known from the ibis cult. As a result, it's possible that visitors did not actually see the mummy for which they had paid; instead, they may have left the burial in the hands of the priests without realising that the dog they had offered as a sacrifice was a puppy rather than one of the healthy adult animals, they had seen inside the Anubieion temple.

It is not certain of the actual time frame during which the catacombs were in use. The number of animals required each year would be too great for them to have all been reared at the Anubieion temple or mummified there. As a result, we can only speculate that the animals may have been raised in a number of 'puppy farms' at Saqqara and in Men-nefer (Memphis). We used the term 'puppy', as already mentioned, with caution because many were just a few days or hours old or younger when they were mummified. It can only be an overall estimate of numbers explained by their tiny size.

It is just dogs that have been discussed so far, and most of the animals in the catacomb are *Canis familiaris*, the domestic dog. But there are a variety of cats, jackals, foxes, and other canines and canine-like animals interred there as well. Also found in these catacombs were two human mummies, both of which were in a very bad state of preservation. This raises questions regarding the connections between human and animal burials.

## What happened to the dogs?
Today, the catacombs' burial galleries are entirely empty, as if they were never used; but enough debris is left to indicate that they formerly held mummies. Naturally, one asks, where did the dogs go? Some of the areas in the catacombs were deliberately cleared out and the mummies could be burned or turned into fertilizer, as seen by an account of shiploads of cat mummies being taken to

Liverpool for sale as fertilizer. Such licenses were frequently granted right into the early twentieth century for the removal of archaeological material for industrial or agricultural purposes. Many of the dog mummies may have suffered from a similar fate.

The Serapeum, where the Apis bulls were interred, and the 3rd Dynasty Step Pyramid of Djoser (c. 2667–2648 BCE) are the two structures that are the most popular attractions at the Saqqara site today. Egyptology and Saqqara were first brought to the public's attention by Auguste Mariette (1821–1881), because of the discovery of the Serapeum in 1851.

Although the Serapeum as we know it dates only from the New Kingdom, the Apis bull is believed to have been buried at Saqqara as early as the 1st Dynasty. The Apis was only the first of many sacred creatures that were eventually buried in Saqqara, though. There is in fact a connection between the animals, the Step Pyramid and the rediscovery of the sacred animal cults of Saqqara.

**Djoser, Imhotep and Professor Emery**
Imhotep, Djoser's principal advisor and the Step Pyramid's architect, is the link that connects the animal cults to the structure. Imhotep is referred to by his titles on a statue base as *'the greatest of seers, the builder, the sculptor, and the maker of stone vases, the Chancellor of the King of Lower Egypt, the first after the King of Upper Egypt, Administrator of the Great Palace, hereditary lord, and the Administrator of the Great Palace.'* This man clearly held a position of power in Djoser's court, and the building of the Step Pyramid solidified his reputation, both during his lifetime and beyond.

Imhotep gained renown as a knowledgeable man and the man who first used stone building. Because of this, he eventually became identified with both Ptah, creator deity, and patron God of Men-nefer, and Thoth, the god of wisdom, writing, and learning. Imhotep took on the persona of a demi-god. There was an obvious link between animal cults and the deified Imhotep, as the Apis was the living image (ba) of Ptah, while the ibis and the baboon were both symbols of Thoth.

But despite the Step Pyramid's fame and Imhotep's own, the location of his tomb was unknown in contemporary times, which is what inspired Professor W. B. Emery (1903–1971) to start looking for his burial place in the 1960s. Despite the fact that his work did not uncover the Tomb of Imhotep, he did find the catacomb where the mothers of the Apis bulls were interred, as well as two burial catacombs for ibises, falcons, baboons, and birds of prey. His research greatly contributed to the resurgence of interest in Saqqara and shed a lot of light on the animal cults that were practised at North Saqqara's Sacred Animal Necropolis (S.A.N.).

If Emery hadn't unexpectedly died while working on the project site in 1971, his work would have undoubtedly produced even better results. The North Ibis Catacomb, which had only recently been discovered at the time of Emery's death, was not further investigated until the 1990s.

## Conclusion

It appears that the Catacombs of Anubis and its once mummified inhabitants are frequently the main centre of fascination for individuals who are interested in animal cults, rather than the temples. The new survey and the faunal research have brought up several intriguing new concerns about how the animals were obtained and mummified, how they were bred, and the relationships between the dedicatees and the animals. It is significant that the catacombs performed many functions over time, illustrating how Egyptian culture, religion, and society also changed.

## Further reading

An in-depth paper was written by Cardiff University on a project that began in 2009, directed by Nicholson with the aim of gaining a more rounded picture of the Dog Catacombs. The paper summarises the work of many individuals with the survey and mapping team led by Dr. Steve Mills (Cardiff University) and the faunal team by Dr. Salima Ikram (American University in Cairo). The intention of this new work has been to refocus research on the animal cults toward the animals themselves, the individuals who operated aspects of the cult and the subterranean structures

associated with them. The temples and shrines, though undeniably significant, are often only the tip of the iceberg, the great bulk being below the waterline, or in this case below ground.
The_Catacombs_of_Anubis_at_North_Saqqara (3).pdf

# Canopic Jars

**Compiled by Judith Page**

Why the ancient Egyptians developed the mummification technique is still a subject of debate. Egyptian cemeteries are to be found usually on the west bank of the Nile Valley, or on the desert's fringes, avoiding the fertile floodplain used for farming.

It is generally accepted from the discovery of naturally desiccated bodies buried in shallow graves in the sand that the Predynastic Period (c. 4000-2960 BCE) gave the ancient Egyptians their concepts of life after death and motivated them to create artificial mummification techniques later in the Dynastic Period (c. 2960 BCE-CE 332).

On the other hand, burials from the Naqada II Period (3650-3300 BCE) in Nekhen/Hierakonpolis have been discovered with a partial wrapping of the body, particularly the head and hands. The presence of pottery pots, slate palettes, and stone beads in burials is typical for this period and this may indicate the religious belief in an afterlife and the wish to preserve the body, rather than the other way around.

Even though the ancient Egyptians accepted physical death, it's possible that they realized that at some level the deceased was still alive, but they were unable to perceive life without the body. They believed that by burying it away from flies and scavenger animals, they were taking care of the body after death. And by making an even bigger effort, the deceased would be more likely to survive. This might explain why graves became brick-lined during the Early Dynastic Period (c. 2960–2649 BCE) or why bodies were wrapped in reed mats. The unfortunate result of this was that the bodies lost contact with the hot, drying sand and began to decay more quickly.

Since the Egyptians did not recognise the significance of the desert sand, they did not return to it. Through much trial and error, even more, extreme preservation procedures had to be created.

Now to the canopic jars. Although Anubis is the best known of the jackal gods, Duamutef may be the one that we most often see. His jackal head features one of the most quintessentially Egyptian artifacts, the canopic jar. A name that has been misappropriated. In ancient Egyptian, they were known as *qebu en wet*, 'jars for embalming', and viscera jars. As we are aware, the ancient Egyptians would pull out the organs prior to the mummification of the body. These organs would be mummified and placed in jars.

Early Egyptologists incorrectly associated the term canopic with the Greek tale of Canopus, the boat captain of Menelaus on the journey to Troy, who 'was buried at Canopus in the Delta where he was revered in the form of a jar'. According to Salima Ikram (Egyptologist) and alternative versions, the name derives from the location Canopus (now Abukir) in the western Nile Delta near Alexandria, where human-headed jars were worshipped as personifications of the god Osiris.

These jars were typically carved from limestone or fashioned or made of pottery. The ancient Egyptians used these jars from the period of the Old Kingdom until the Late Period or Ptolemaic Period. The viscera were simply wrapped and deposited alongside the body, and not stored as they were in a single canopic jar.

The oldest example is that of the 4th Dynasty Queen Hetepheres (c. 2575-2465 BCE) at Giza, which consisted of a plain square box made of Egyptian alabaster with four compartments and a lid. The earliest jar version is that of Merysankh III of the same Dynasty, also at Giza, and these appeared with heads, possibly representing the deceased person, in the Middle Kingdom (c. 2030-1802 BCE).

Canopic jar designs evolved over time. The oldest were made of stone or wood and originate from the 11th and 12th Dynasties. The most recent jars were from the New Kingdom. In the Old Kingdom these jars had plain lids, but during the First Intermediate Period, they appeared with human heads and were said to represent the deceased. The jar coverings were sometimes modelled after (or painted to look like) the head of Anubis, the deity of death and embalming. By the late Eighteenth Dynasty, canopic jars had come to depict Horus' four sons.

Old Kingdom canopic jars were infrequently engraved and had a simple lid. Inscriptions became more common in the Middle Kingdom, and lids were often shaped like human heads. By the Middle Kingdom the internal organs were put under the protection of one of the Four Sons of Horus and in the New Kingdom (c. 1550-1070 BCE) the jars took on the heads of these gods.

They were as follows:
Hapi, the baboon-headed god representing the North, whose jar contained the lungs and was protected by the goddess Nephthys. Hapi is often used interchangeably with the Nile god Hapi, though they are actually different gods.

Duamutef, the jackal-headed god representing the East, whose jar contained the stomach and was protected by the goddess Neith.

Imsety, the human-headed god representing the South, whose jar contained the liver and was protected by the goddess Isis.

Qebehsenuef, the falcon-headed god representing the West, whose jar contained the intestines and was protected by the goddess Serqet.

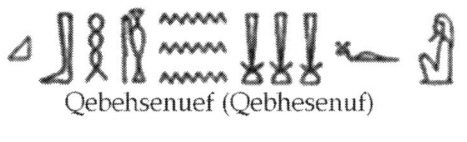

There was no jar for the heart as the Egyptians considered it to be the seat of the soul and hence it was left inside the body.

'Thoth recites your liturgy,
And calls you with his spells;
The Sons of Horus guard your body,
And daily bless your ka.'

Early canopic jars were buried in tombs with the deceased's sarcophagus inside a canopic chest. Occasionally they were found to be set in rows either at the four corners of the chamber or beneath the bier. After the early periods, the exteriors of the jars had inscriptions that were occasionally lengthy and complicated. An inscription from the Saïte or Ptolemaic period cited by the Egyptologist, Sir Wallace Budge, begins, *'Thy bread is to thee. Thy beer is to thee. Thou livest upon that on which Ra_lives.'* Other inscriptions tell of purification in the afterlife.

Dummy canopic jars were introduced in the Third Intermediate Period and later. Improved embalming techniques permitted the viscera to be preserved in the body; traditional jars remained a component of tombs but were no longer hollowed out for organ storage. Many jars were made, and surviving examples may be seen in museums all over the world.

Under a 2,600-year-old stone wall, a 30-meter-deep trench that formerly contained the secrets of a fascinating and thriving embalmment workshop was being finished. At the base of the Unas pyramid, a new entombment chamber was found under the sands of the Saqqara necropolis. Additionally, the coffin of a woman by the name of Didibastet has emerged, and with a mystery within: she was covered with six canopic vessels, defying the conventional design of four vessels, where the organs of the deceased were preserved.

Ramadan Badri Husein, overseer of the German-Egyptian mission of the University of Tübingen, renowned for his many discoveries within the area of the Saqqara graveyard, said in a statement to the local news agency, 'Its six canopic vessels are a genuine astonishment because the custom comprised of removing, preserving and putting away the lungs, stomach or spleen, liver and digestive organs in four holders.'

It would be interesting to know which other gods were chosen as heads on the additional two jars.

ACT scan revealed that the jars contained human tissue, implying that Didibastet's mummification may have been the result of a special request. (illust. 39)

# Dark Journey of the Soul

**Compiled by Judith Page**

In ancient Egypt, only a fraction of the population was literate, few could access the Book of the Dead reproduced on tomb walls, and still fewer had access to the papyrus manuscripts. It was the elite of Egyptian society, the pharaohs, and nobles that had strong beliefs regarding the afterlife, but possession of a soul and expectation of immortality depended on social status. Many people were forgotten after their deaths. So, we are looking at two elitist funerary religions, since in Egypt the elite was based on social class. However, there did occur in Egypt what J. Edward Wright refers to in his book *The Early History of Heaven* as the democratisation of heaven, where this private knowledge of the afterlife gradually passed down from pharaoh exclusivity with the Pyramid Texts, to monarch exclusivity with the Coffin Texts, and finally to larger accessibility with the economical Book of the Dead.

The afterlife for ancient peoples occupied a central focus in their thoughts and beliefs. Not only that, but it also played a key role in their daily lives, as every moment was a preparatory movement toward that final journey. According to William Brede Kristensen, '[these] people were possessed more by thoughts about death than thoughts about life. Clearly, the Egyptian kings like all Egyptians were more concerned about their dwellings in the afterlife than those in this life.' For the ancient Egyptians, the afterlife journey was not some imaginative vision, serving more as a didactic allegory or instructive narrative, but a serious reality.

To the Egyptians, death was viewed as both the great enemy and the sublime liberator, conferring upon the deceased eternal life, as well as admission into the paradisical fields of the afterlife. For them, the idea of cosmic immortality was no mere metaphor, but a true destination to be reached via an arduous route of distractions, penalties, and gateways.

Immortality was not granted to the deceased because he or she lived a moral life while here on earth. The deceased was required to know certain information, even to memorise it; also, to be prepared accordingly before death—all this resulting in how to successfully enter the paradisical fields of immortality. Unlike today the afterlife was an active event, instead of passive ideology.

For ancient peoples of Egypt, the afterlife, and their place in it offered a possible setting for their future. The journey of a soul through the afterlife was not merely some imaginative flight of fancy or speculative conjecture, but a living part of the cultural milieu.

The cults of the afterlife flourished in ancient Egypt and were a prominent aspect of the community. Their beliefs dominated architecture and religious philosophy and culminated in ritual burials.

Egyptian death cults offered spells, rituals, and passwords for successfully traversing the afterlife and both propounded penalties for failing to perform these actions at the proper time. These ancient people emphasised their conduct and behaviour after death, as opposed to the moral scrutiny placed upon our corporeal lives in modern-day society.

It is safe to assume that the ancient Egyptians, though veiled at first glance, concentrated on their relationship in the myths of Osiris in the underworld.

In addition to these myths, specific texts were prepared to help facilitate the deceased's passage through the afterlife. Ritual burial and preparation of the dead body played a key role, including the mummification process. We see an emphasis placed on the conduct of the deceased's burial, instead of a concern for how they lived their life, morally speaking, which is the dominant pattern of today.

It was important to these ancient peoples, to exert a greater command over every day conduct and suggest the superiority of death over one's life experiences.

Being situated along the mighty river Nile, Egyptian society regularly awaited the annual overflowing of its banks for the purposes of agriculture and farming. For the Egyptians, this was seen as an act of fertility, the upsurge of water saturating the parched, receptive earth and generating new life for the crops and plant life. So, for the Egyptians, the sky, Nut, was a woman, while Earth, Geb, was a man since the earth carried the Nile flood.

Above all, one thing is certain of this ancient society: they were more pre-occupied with thoughts about death than thoughts about life. And they upheld a belief in the divine nature of deceased human beings.

For them, death had a double meaning. In some respects, it was their enemy, and likewise, it was the source of their eternal life. The reasoning for their preoccupation with the subject is clear.

Even the Nile's yearly flooding, which brought both life through the crops and death from the perilous floods, had a dual significance for them. One of the primary deities linked to the afterlife and the deceased was Osiris, king of the underworld. Due to the well-known tale of his brother Set plotting to have him killed, cut apart, and distributed, he had already experienced death and resurrection.

But he was then put back together via the mummification process and brought to life by his wife Isis, at which point he assumed rule over the underworld. *'Look: I have found you lying on your side, O completely inert one! My sister, said Isis to Nephthys, it is our brother. Come that we may lift up his head! Come that we may reassemble his bones! ... Let this not remain inert in our hands! ... Osiris, live, Osiris! May the completely inert one who is on his side rise. I am Isis.'*

Many cults were formed around this crucial figure, and when the deceased was faced with his journey in the underworld it was necessary for him to identify himself as Osiris, which we find in the Egyptian Book of the Dead.

The aspect of the being which embarked upon this journey was even known as the Osiris-Soul. Therefore, identification with the king, Osiris was critical for the deceased to survive the underworld. And such identification, or spells, needed vociferation because for the Egyptians the spoken word was seen as magical; it was the ordering component out of which chaos was forced into a logical order. The word is what causes the divine act of creation, of giving life.

Thus, the infinite spirit was seen as ordering creation out of formlessness and chaos. With this kind of magical protection, principally as laid down in funerary texts such as The Book of the Dead (New Kingdom 1540-1075 B.C.E.), recently deceased souls could reach Aaru, or the Field of Reeds, the Egyptian version of Heaven or Paradise.

Other predominant Egyptian deities included Ra, the sun god, and then his opposite, the symbol of evil incarnate known as the Apep snake. Due to the annual shedding of its skin, this snake was seen as a symbol of death and renewal, like Osiris. However, unlike Osiris, this snake lacked the quality of resurrection, which gave the living the opportunity to survive death by virtue of his mere being. Furthermore, Ra's opponent was particularly mentioned as being the Apep snake.

Like Ra, the dead man travels during the night across the back of Apep and defeats the snake, be it in the depth of the Kingdom of Death or at the eastern horizon. Another prescribed formula for the deceased to emerge victorious from their afterlife journey was to utter the words time and time again to the many foes of the underworld, including Apep, as cited in funerary texts: *'I am the sun god Ra, Atum, Khepera'*.

Both Osiris and Ra were seen as separate and yet interconnected, as Egyptian cosmology and myth are far from being consistent. One reason for this may be attributed to the fact that Ra and Osiris were in the underworld at night when Ra was riding his solar disk from west to east, preparing to arise again with the dawn.

For the ancient Egyptians, burial rituals and symbolically cartographic hieroglyphs were very important when burying their deceased. As discussed, this began with the act of mummification, in which the dead body was bound up with cloth.

Symbolically, the bandages or cloth represented the magical knot, seen in some images as looking like the mathematical infinity symbol, recognisable as the numerical figure 8 laying on its side, also called a lemniscate in algebraic geometry.

This symbol was often placed inside the hand of the deceased, to indicate the resurrection of both man and gods in the universal life. By binding the entire body in this symbolic cloth, it is possible the priests were hoping to wrap up the deceased within the folds of eternity.

Other items of importance included the Canopic Jars which held the deceased's organs, as already discussed. Once the deceased was prepared and placed into his elaborate death chamber, the journey of the afterlife began in earnest. His soul exited the tomb in the form of an incarnated bird known as the Ba-bird. (illust. 40)

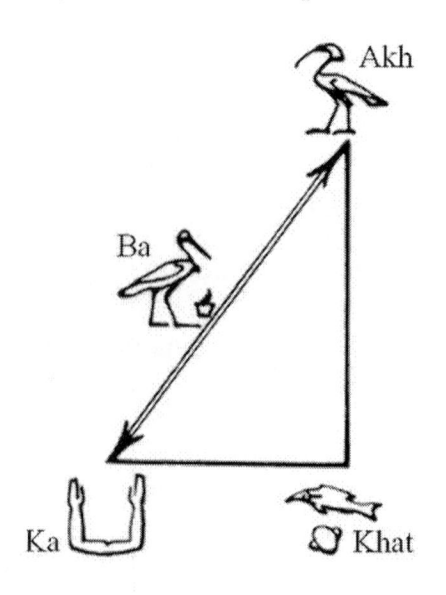

The soul was not viewed by the Egyptians as a single, cohesive entity. The Ka, Ba, and Akh were instead divided into three significant elements that made up the immortal soul. The Ka is each person's source of life. It is stated that the Ka enters the body and gives it life as soon as Khnum has finished molding the body out of clay and is immortal and identical to that person.

*Khnum fashioning a human on his potters wheel (Luxor Temple)* (illust. 41)

The Ka ensures that a person will live on after death, but it does require nourishment. The energy from food offerings left by the living can be absorbed by this portion of the soul. In the expectation that the Ka will be fed and watered if the living doesn't leave any offerings, food and drink representations are frequently painted inside tombs.

Some priests would cast rituals to induce a god to grant the Ka loaves of bread or beer. After death, the Ka would usually remain in the tomb, and many ancient Egyptians would place miniature figurines in the tomb to encourage it to stay, giving it something tangible to possess if the corpse was injured.

The Ba was thought to be a more 'mobile' component of the soul because it was able to leave both the afterlife and the tomb during the day. It would resemble a huge bird and have the deceased person's head on it. The Ba was thought to be a symbol of the person's heart and would house their individuality.

When the Ba left the safety of the tomb, it needed to be cautious as if it were to be damaged in any way, it wouldn't remember where to return to, and that part of the soul would be destroyed as it wandered aimlessly evermore.

The Akh would be the immortal soul's third and final component. This area of the soul is little understood. Some people think that this is the portion of the soul that will, hopefully, travel to the Field of Reeds in the hereafter.

According to Wafaa El Saddik (Egyptologist), in *Egypt: The World of the Pharaohs,* this is the part we would most closely identify with our current definition of an immortal soul. Some people think that the Ba and Ka can only unite to create the Akh and that the area of the soul that deals with religion are completely different from the rest of the soul.

Anubis was said to have guided the souls, to ensure they did not become lost in the underworld. When a person died, at least a part of their soul (most likely the Akh) would travel to the underworld, also known as Amduat, for judgement.

There were two stages to the judgement process for ancient Egyptians. The first test was measuring the subject's heart against Ma'at in the Hall of Truth. Osiris would oversee judging the heart's weight. The heart is on one end of the scale. A solitary feather from Ma'at was on the other. Ma'at was the goddess of many different concepts, including harmony, justice, balance, and truth.

If a person's heart was equivalent to or lighter than one of Ma'at's feathers, then they lived a life full of what she represents and pass the first judgement. If a person's heart was heavier than a feather, they were condemned. Egyptians were unaware of hell and eternal suffering.

Those that failed were instead devoured by Ammit. She was the devourer of the worthless dead; a hideous creature composed of a lion, hippopotamus, and crocodile parts. Those who were consumed by this beast ceased to exist. They would experience neither rebirth nor eternal life. Those who survived the weighing and Ammit's judgement were next judged by 42 gods.

According to the Egyptian Book of the Dead, the goal was to accompany Ra in his solar barque and enter into the cyclic circle of the sun, thus transcending death and then, seemingly, entering the Field of Reeds. Not before numerous trials and obstacles were situated in the way. Most notably, the negative confessions, chapter 125 of the Book of the Dead.

The goal of this line of questioning is to give the deceased a chance to reveal his virtue and assume the title of Osiris, only conferred upon those who go forward into immortality, as Osiris did before them. Therefore, throughout the Book of the Dead, the soul is always referred to as Osiris. (illust. 42)

Instead, a complex journey awaited, filled with dangers and challenges, to which the deceased was subjected. This became the most important aspect of the afterlife, which the ancient Egyptian people expressed in every aspect of their society and culture.

Ultimately, for them, the destination of their journey through the afterlife was the resurrection and eternal life in the Field of Reeds where once and for all they entered the kingdom of the gods, not merely as faithful subjects but truly as one of them, and one of the immortal divinities who could never die.

Sadly, we have no scientific methodology available to determine whether or not this is the case, and so visionary speculation, unfortunately, is one of the few means we currently have at our disposal.

For that crucial occasion, dedication, expertise, focus, and research called for the highest level of solemnity. The afterlife had a significant part in this culture, as is shown in their iconography, ceremonial literature, and burial structures. According to the content of the Egyptian Book of the Dead, it can be inferred that these ancient peoples placed more emphasis on their conduct and afterlife behaviour than the moral scrutiny modern culture places on physical activities. One would question why these cultures placed such a high value on the afterlife, why it was more essential than life itself, and why it was to be taken literally given the wealth of archaeological evidence they left behind.

We are reminded that this idea is not going away, and that mankind is unlikely to give up its belief that there is a meaningful existence that follows physical death by the persistence and universality of heaven and the afterlife in humanity's worldview.

We may not be ready for the global repercussions of losing faith in the existence of the hereafter. It is feasible to imagine a society that has completely abandoned post-mortem aspirations and is obsessively consumed with material existence and material possessions. However, when these worldly possessions dwindle, a war for resources would break out. So, something must be held high to inspire us to move away from total materialism. Nothing would be more regrettable than to finish this life only to discover that there were many gates, tests, perils, and rehearsed recitals waiting for us on the other side.

The ancient Egyptian idea of the afterlife is vastly different from what many believe today. Most people today believe that their life will be judged upon their death. If they are judged to have done well by their religion's standards, then they are admitted into a paradise. If they have not done well, then the possibility of eternal punishment awaits them, often in a fiery realm.

Some religions do believe in a halfway realm—not quite a punishment but not quite paradise either. Others believe in reincarnation, where the soul of the deceased returns to be reborn into a new life on Earth. For the Egyptians, things were not quite that simple.

ANUBIS ~ an INNER GUIDE

# From Anubis to Saint Christopher

**Compiled by Judith Page**

As Christianity took hold of Egypt's religious landscape, the earlier Egyptian religion went into decline. Since the Egyptian animal cults were last documented around AD 340, it is safe to assume that this was the end of the active worship of jackal gods. (illust. 43)

At least in name, the older jackal gods remained. In Christian magical literature from Egypt, Anubis (together with Isis, Osiris, and Horus) was occasionally invoked. There are Greek and Coptic papyri mentioning the names 'Anoup' and 'Anoub' (the most prevalent of which), long after the god's cult had died out.

The jackal gods' images endured. In Eastern Christian icons, depictions of saints, most notably St. Christopher, with human bodies and dog heads appear to have been inspired by earlier Egyptian depictions of the jackal-headed gods.

St. Christopher, who died as a martyr, is one of the most venerated Christian saints. However, like the lives of many saints, he is often shrouded in mystery. The truth is that we don't even know if St

Christopher existed in the first place. (illust. 44)

This mystery is only deepened because of an amazing discovery made when visiting the Byzantine Museum of Athens, Greece. St. Christopher with a Dog's Head is shown in this icon. Why does St. Christopher have a dog's head on his shoulders? What Does Jackal God Anubis have in common with St. Christopher?

It's interesting that the holy Christian bears a striking resemblance to the Egyptian god Anubis, the Jackal of the Dead. As we have already learned, Anubis was the guardian of the dead in the underworld. While many called him 'Lord of the Pure Land', his title of 'Lord of the Holy Land' signified his authority over the desert's many cemeteries. Another possible meaning of his title is the jackal deity, who would guard over graves in the desert from atop a sacred mountain. (illust. 45)

For example, in the Pyramid Texts, 'the Jackal, Governor of the Bows' appears, with nine bows represented as real bows, most likely depicting Egyptian foes.

In the Catholic Church, he is the patron saint of bachelors, transportation, travelling, storms, epilepsy, gardeners, holy death, and toothache. It has long puzzled historians, artists and scholars why St. Christopher is represented with a dog's head and a child resting on his shoulder and a staff in his other hand. St. Christopher is often represented as a giant of a man. (illust.46)

Early translations did not always render an accurate translation of the Greek term kunokephalos, 'dog-headed', and at times translated it as canineus, 'dog-like'. This progressively morphed to read 'Canaanite' (Cananeus) since it seemed apparent that a Saint could not really have been 'dog-like'.

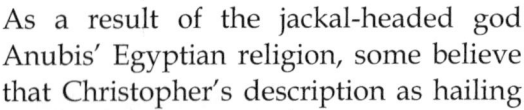

As a result of the jackal-headed god Anubis' Egyptian religion, some believe that Christopher's description as hailing from the country of the dog-headed originated in this way.

Those in the Greco-Roman era were accustomed to labelling people who lived outside of civilisation as cannibals and dog-headed people, according to some scholars. In other words, the original author of the St. Christopher legend was merely using cultural metaphor when he stated that St. Christopher came from a world of cannibals and dog-headed people.

**The Mysterious Dog-Headed Race**
An ancient tale mentions a mysterious dog-headed race that once lived among men. According to the Orthodox Arts Journal, 'dog-headed men appear in the story of St-Mercurios, a warrior saint whose father was eaten by two dog-headed men later converted by St. Mercurios. This saint could unleash the vicious nature of these dog-headed individuals on the enemies of the Roman empire in a manner akin to how Romans and later Christians utilised Barbarians in their own conflicts.'

It was widely held in Medieval times that there were many other races, among them the Cynocephalus, or dog-headed people. German poet and playwright Walter of Speyer depicted St. Christopher as a human-eating, dog-barking cynocephalic behemoth in the Chananean land. St. Christopher is not the only example of dog-headed men appearing in iconography. They are also depicted in representations of Pentecost, most in Armenian texts, but also in Western artwork.

Christopher is one of the saints of Christian antiquity about whom little verifiable information is known. According to Father William, "tradition holds that he died at Lycia on the southern coast of Asia Minor about the year 251. Various legends surround his life. The most popular is that he was a rather ugly, giant man, born to a heathen king who was married to a Christian, who had prayed to the Blessed Mother for a child. Originally named Offerus, he carried people across the river for his livelihood. He converted from paganism through the teaching of a hermit named Babylas. Christopher believed that our Lord was the most powerful of all, more powerful than any man and one whom even Satan feared."

One day, again according to the legend, Christopher picked up an insignificant passenger — a small child. 'As they proceeded [across the river],' wrote Father William, 'the child kept growing heavier and Christopher feared that they would drown. The child then revealed himself as Jesus, and the heaviness was due to the weight of the world that he carried on his shoulders.'

**But did St. Christopher really exist?**
It's going to take a lot of work to figure out how St. Christopher lived and died. We have no idea who he really is. Tradition holds that this intriguing man lived during the Roman emperor Decius' (249-251CE) Christian persecutions and was martyred by the governor of Antioch, this is according to historical evidence based on legend.

Historian David Woods writes: 'Peter of Attalia may have carried St. Christopher's relics to Alexandria, where he may have been connected with Egyptian martyr St. Means'.

St. Christopher appears in Orthodox belief as the warrior Cynocephalus from Lycea, and in art as a dog-headed man in the icon of the saint. He can also grow to monstrous proportions on occasion. Another tale tells of him being a Roman soldier kidnapped from the farthest reaches of the earth, who converted and was martyred by an Emperor.

Whoever he was, this holy man gave his life rather than offer up his body as an offering to the pagan deities. He was assassinated on the king's orders. Attempts were made to decapitate Christopher, but all failed. Before his death, St. Christopher had converted thousands of people to Christianity. The 25th of July is his feast day.

## A giant among men

St. Christopher figures prominently in a story from the Middle Ages that describes giants as a race that once roamed Europe. People who saw St. Christopher had a different narrative to tell, despite modern stories portraying him as an ordinary man or even a slightly homely one.

Those who knew him said he belonged to a dog-headed, cannibalistic tribe of giants. Jacques de Voragine described St. Christopher in *The Golden Legend* as having a 'terrifying mien' and standing twelve coudees tall. A measurement equal to or greater than a foot in length is called a coudee. According to this old legend, St. Christopher weighed between 12 and 18 stone (a fact that has become hidden in or even erased from church history).

In contrast to Western iconography, Eastern churches' depictions of St. Christopher are more accurate. Historical sources frequently imply that St. Christopher was the result of a sexual encounter between a human and the Egyptian god Anubis, a creature based on the Greek Anoubis, which came from the Egyptians jackal-headed god who was believed to lead the dead to judgment.

The legend of Saint Christopher quite clearly states that he was a giant. Not just a tall man, but a genuine giant. As the story goes, it was his size that enabled him to easily transport the Christ child across a river and thereby secured his place as the patron saint of travellers - that is, until the Church decided that the evidence for Christopher's very existence was entirely legendary and decanonised him.

Nonetheless, he remains a popular though unofficial saint, and his image is fixed in our cultural psyche. It has been speculated that St. Christopher could be the same man known as the Coptic Saint Menas for whom a 4$^{th}$ century burial site is known. Doubts about the historical existence of Christopher, long the patron saint of travellers, prompted the Catholic Church to remove his name from the calendar of saints in 1969. (illust. 47)

**De-canonised**
The saint's name means 'Christ-bearer'.
There have been many millions of individuals around the world wearing Saint Christopher medals on their necks, in their bags, and on the dashboards of their cars. He had been a household name for hundreds of years and was much revered, but in 1969 Saint Christopher was officially demoted as the patron saint of travellers. However, the tale surrounding him was simply too alluring to ignore. This image of him carrying Jesus across a raging torrent in his arms was comforting to many non-flyers when the aircraft seat belt indicator came on. Then suddenly, he was crossed off the A-list.

Or was he?

It was not just Saint Christopher who was downgraded, a number of other early Church saints experienced a reassignment. When Pope Paul VI altered the Liturgical Calendar, which contains the feast days of saints that are celebrated at Mass, confusion occurred.

Pope Paul was following a directive from Vatican II, that was outlined in the council's constitution on the liturgy, Sacrosanctum Concilium.

The issue was that there were simply too many saints on the calendar, especially those who had a more regional or localised following than a global one. They said: 'In order to avoid a conflict between commemorating religious figures and those who commemorate the mysteries of salvation, some feasts should remain within a particular Christian community or nation; only those that commemorate universally significant saints should be shared by all Christians.' (SC 111).

The council 'examined the calendar and removed those saints whose historical base was more grounded on tradition than provable fact, changed the feast days to coincide with the anniversary of a saint's death or martyrdom whenever possible, and added saints that were recently canonized and had universal Church appeal,' wrote Father William Saunders, the dean of the Notre Dame Graduate School of Christendom College. 'Moreover, local conferences of bishops could add to the universal calendar those saints important to the faithful in their own country'.

Even though Christopher's name was removed from the new Liturgical Calendar, the rumours that he had died were grossly exaggerated. In the eyes of the Roman Catholic Church, he has always been a saint. His ancestry and legend tell a story in and of itself. His popularity grew during the Middle Ages, and he became one of the '14 Holy Helpers': a group of saints celebrated on 8th August in southern Germany, Austria, and northern Italy. (illust. 48)

So don't get rid of that medallion; the long-celebrated 'Christ-bearer' can still get you home safely.

# Man's Best Friend

**Compiled by Judith Page**

The question of whether the dog was domesticated by humans or whether it self-domesticated is now being discussed in the scientific community. No matter what the circumstances are, dogs have a greater capacity than any other creature to comprehend how to peacefully cohabit with human beings.

The dog's personality has made an unforgettable mark on us, as seen by the many tales and traditions that have been passed down through the generations. Even those who considered it impossible for the dog to be redeemed were typically forced to acknowledge at some point that it did have some admirable qualities.

Throughout history, the dog has been elevated to a position of honour and reverence by many people. Some recent research suggests that the human-canine link could date back 100,000 years during which dogs have been an important part of human life. 'Opener of the path', as the Egyptian god Wepwawet's name implies, is a fitting description of the dog.

For countless æons, man and dog have been hunting and campfire companions. There is no doubt that dogs have been a part of our culture for a very long time. In addition to being family pets, they were sometimes used as battle dogs.

'Iwiw' was the Egyptian name for dog, alluding to its bark. This may explain why dogs were used to guard people, places, homes, and temples in ancient Egypt.

## ANUBIS ~ an INNER GUIDE

Archaeologists from Egypt's Supreme Council of Antiquities were alerted, and they estimated that the earliest drawings in the cave dated back to around 7000 BCE; they portray men and women, armed with bows, hunting with tamed dogs. The Nile Valley is home to numerous prehistoric depictions of human-dog hunting situations.

Predynastic Egyptian texts contain the earliest mentions of dogs. As far back as the fifth millennium BCE, dog bones have been unearthed in Egypt, and a household pottery piece known as the 'Moscow Cup' from the Badarian Culture shows the first known depiction of domesticated dogs. (illust. 49)

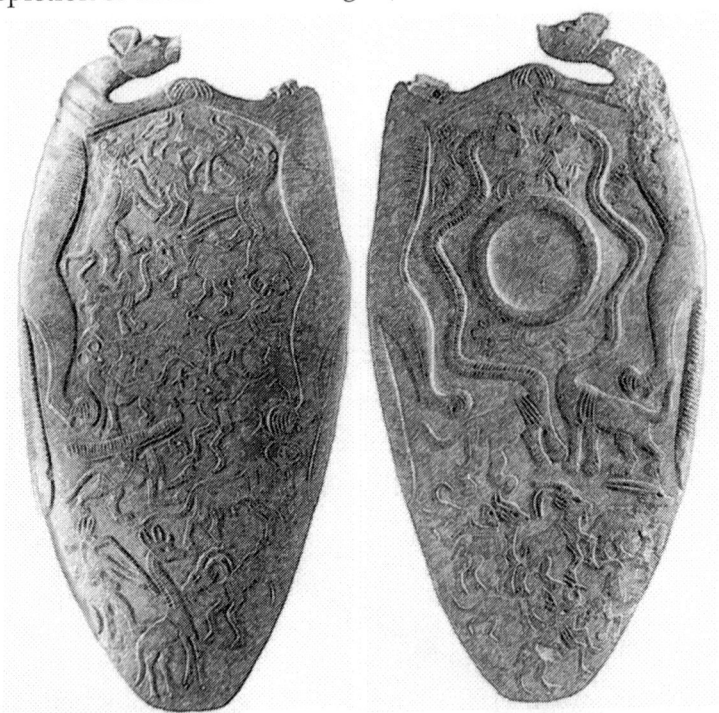

In both the Ashmolean Palette and the Hunting Palette, we have natural depictions of dogs with collars. These palettes were made during the Naqada II period (3500-3000 BCE). However, there are several depictions of domesticated dogs in ancient Egyptian murals dating all the way back to the Old Kingdom.

Invaders of Egypt known as the Hyksos, who ruled from Avaris in the Delta, are thought to have popularised the use of spike-collared dogs in battle. During the New Kingdom, the expansionist Pharaoh Rameses II, who was known to yell "havoc and let slip the dogs of war", frequently employed these fast and light battle-chariots. War dogs were used by earlier dynasties, but perhaps not to the extent witnessed later.

Because Egypt does not appear to have possessed any wolves that could have been domesticated, the first dogs may have been brought in from elsewhere during the pre-dynastic period, which could indicate the degree of trade that existed in the Mediterranean region at the time.

Before unification, an 11th Dynasty tomb stela depicting Horus Wah-ankh Intef II and his hounds (all of whom had Berber names) shows the king with canines imported from the West, whereas Hatshepsut brought dogs with her from Punt. A dog was one of the animals sent to Pharaoh Ramses II by the Nubians as a tribute. (illust. 50)

The Sloughi and Saluki, two of the world's oldest dog breeds, were popular in Egypt at various points in its history. With their trumpet-shaped tails, these animals were common in Egypt during the Old Kingdom. While short-legged dogs became popular in Egypt's Middle Kingdom under the 5th dynasty, the New Kingdom Egyptians preferred a breed called a 'fleet harrier', which had upright ears in the pre-dynastic period but lopped them by the Old Kingdom. They were said to be 'swifter than the harrier and faster than the shadow' because of their incredible speed. (illust. 51)

The dogs buried in dog cemeteries in later times were mostly slim and medium-sized, but several enormous mastiffs and small spitz-type dogs were also found buried in these cemeteries.

Selective breeding occurred almost as soon as dogs were domesticated in ancient Egypt, but not to the extent that compulsive breeding is practised today, which is a relatively contemporary invention dating only to the Middle Ages.

As a result of this, the Egyptians were able to breed canines that had distinct characteristics from their native African and Middle Eastern populations. Some dog breeds were so highly esteemed that they could only be owned by Egypt's nobles, as is still the case today among dog lovers.

To be a treasured family pet, a dog didn't have to be pure bred back then, as it is now. It is true that in ancient Egypt, the term 'mutt' and 'mongrel' was used, but they were far better cared for because even the lowest of breeds were believed descended from Anubis, the god of the underworld.

Unlike other animals, dogs were given names like family members. Some Egyptian dog names were human names, exactly like the ones we give our own pets today. 'Abu', the Egyptian word for 'bow-wow', was a common name for a dog.

Many of the ancient Egyptian dog names can be deduced from their leather collars, stela, and wall reliefs. 'Good Herdsman', 'North Wind', 'Brave-One', 'Reliable', and even 'Useless' were among their many choices. The colour of the dog inspired names like 'Blacky', while a number like 'the Fifth' was given to others. There were also names that conveyed a sense of affection, while others referred to the dog's characteristics or skills. (illust. 52)

It is still possible for dogs to be harmed by their status as 'servants' of the human species. In ancient literature, prisoners are referred to as 'the king's dogs'. Whilst it may be true for religious purposes that cats were the most honoured of animals in Egypt, for example

in the worship of the cat goddess Bastet, and for practical use, such as pest control; according to Diodorus Siculus:
*'Cats were so clever they fooled us gullible humans into believing them sacred'.*
He goes on to describe the people's anger when particular animals were killed:
*'The killer of a cat, or dog or an ibis has to die, whether he killed the animal on purpose or by mistake; a crowd gathers and without any decision of a judge they maltreat the perpetrator in the cruellest way.'*

Herodotus describes how the Egyptians mourned the death of a family cat or dog:
*'In every house that a cat has died those who dwell in that house shave their eyebrows, but those in which a dog has died must shave their whole body and also their head.'*

It was also illegal to kill a dog in Egypt. If you did so, the penalty was death! (illust. 53)

It is possible that dogs have surpassed cats as the most cherished household pets for the simple reason that they are more human-like in terms of their temperament, desires, and aspirations. One difference between cats and dogs is that it is rare for a cat to welcome its master home after a long day of labour, but quite normal for dogs.

It goes without saying that the Egyptians revered cats, but chose dogs as companions and hunting partners, and many owners had the mummies of their dogs accompanying them in their tombs to ensure that the relationship between master and dog endured even after death.

Near the graves of ladies, archers, and dwarfs, a section of the Abydos cemetery was set aside for dogs. A large number of dog

cemeteries and dog mummies, particularly in the vicinity of the ancient city of Hardai (the Greeks referred to it as Cynopolis or 'Dog City'), serve as silent witnesses to the intimate link of attachment between dogs and their masters.
In 1938, Dr. G. A. Reisner who had been excavating in Egypt with the Harvard-Boston Expedition, found an inscription recording the burial of a greyhound-like dog named *Abuwtiyuw*, with all the ritual ceremonies of a great man of Egypt carried out by the King of Upper and Lower Egypt:
*'His Majesty ordered that his guard dog Abuwtiyuw be given a coffin from the royal treasury, fine linen in great quantity, incense, perfumed ointment and that a tomb be built for him by the gang of masons. His Majesty did this for him in order that he might be honoured.'*

Other cities like Hardai where dogs were lovingly buried were considered sacred to the dog-god Anubis. Like the dogs who honoured him, he was a friend of mankind.

There was little respect for dogs beyond Egypt, despite Bible references to dogs such as the greyhound, that praised their virtues. (Proverbs 30:29-31, King James Version). Judeo-Christian literature portrays them as scavengers who prey on the weak. Even to this day in Islam, dogs are considered filthy creatures.

Iraq, Jordan and Iran are currently engaged in what amounts to 'holy war against dogs' as evidenced by recent events. Every day, government agents round up and kill dozens of dogs. Dog ownership is only practiced illegally by the more affluent members of society.

Thousands of dogs are 'put down' in North America and Europe, not because of any religious conviction, but because it is more convenient, such as around vacation time, and the pretext of 'public health' is frequently used. In the Far East dogs as well as cats are on the menu – but we won't go down that road.

When greyhounds retire from racing, they are often abused and killed in gruesome ways. If no philanthropic organisations can save them, they will be made into dog chow. If the ancient Egyptians were around today, they would certainly not understand the maltreatment dogs are accorded in this modern world of ours, and neither would man's best friend.

It's possible that the only conclusion we can reach with any degree of certainty is that the ancient Egyptians adored their canine companions and, in turn, were showered with unwavering affection from them. In the eyes of a dog, the human who cared for it was their best friend, from the lowest Egyptian to the mightiest of Pharaohs. Dogs don't lie, and they don't judge — but what about Anubis?

The Panchen Lama was said to have had two such dogs that accompanied him everywhere and were attended to by the religious prime minister and high priest. Each dog also had its own retinue of servants.

In both Tibet and China, lion dogs, or statues of these dogs, also served as sacred guardians of temples.

The affection for toy dogs that was prevalent among the royal families of Europe may be traced back to at least the 15th century. During this time period, paintings of the French royal court frequently included the Papillion, sometimes known as the butterfly dog.

The Bichon Frise became a common sight at the French royal court during the reign of Francis I (1515–1547). It is also stated that Henry III had such a deep affection for these canines that he fashioned a basket that could be worn around his neck in order to transport his pets.

Large coursing hounds were commonly kept by European royalty in ancient times. Even the legendary King Arthur had a hunting dog named Caval, which translates as 'horse' in Latin. However, the aristocratic courts of Renaissance Europe were no places for these large breeds.

The King Charles Spaniel got its name from King Charles II of England, who favoured the breed over any other dog. The current

Queen Elizabeth II had a fondness for Welsh corgis, and the dogs frequently accompanied her when she made public appearances. (illust. 54)

Princess Elizabeth and her father King George VI with their corgis.

ANUBIS ~ an INNER GUIDE

# PART II

# Saint Roch and His Dog

**Compiled by Judith Page**

Saint Roch, also known as Saint Rocco, was the son of the city's prosperous governor in Montpellier, France. He was an only child and was born with a dark red cross-shaped birthmark on his chest. This his mother took as a sign that the Blessed Virgin Mary had heard and answered her prayers to be healed of her barrenness.

As a child, Saint Roch, like his parents, was a devout Catholic, fasting twice a week. On the death of his parents in his twentieth year, Saint Roch distributed all his worldly goods among the poor, as did Francis of Assisi. And although his father on his deathbed had ordained him as Governor of Montpellier, he nevertheless set out penniless on a pilgrimage to Rome's holy sites.

St Roch was content to be free from all earthly constraints and it led him to join the Third Order Franciscans and to wear the recognisable pilgrim's hat and cloak, a sign of piety.

When he arrived at Acquapendente, a little town near Viterbo, he witnessed the devastation brought on by the black plague that at the time was ravaging Europe. Despite the dangers of contracting this deadly disease, he spent time there, tending to the sick in both their homes and hospitals. Many people were cured just by Saint Roch making the Sign of the Cross over them, and curiously, at no time was he ever infected.

He continued his charity work in the village until the disease had stopped spreading further, after which he continued his pilgrimage. Every plague-infested town he travelled through on his journey to Rome was witness to his amazing power of healing, which included Rome itself.

During his travels while in Piacenza, he eventually succumbed to the debilitating condition, having contracted it in his leg. Instead of burdening anyone else with his illness, he gave thanks to God and prepared to die in a secluded forest hut far from civilisation. But it was not meant to be. Fortunately, a neighbouring nobleman's hunting dog found him and brought him food every day, licking his wounds and snuggling next to him to keep him warm. Near where Saint Roch lay, a spring arose to provide the saint with fresh water. (illust. 55)

The nobleman, out of curiosity, followed his dog to the woods one day which led him to discover and further aid the holy pilgrim. Saint Roch's health began to improve, and he received divine guidance that he should return to Montpellier, the place where he grew up.

When Saint Roch arrived in his birth town, he discovered a city at war. He was approached by soldiers asking who he was but he refused to disclose his true identity, that he was the son of the former governor.

His ambiguity raised suspicions and he was accused of being a spy. Saint Roch did not defend himself against these accusations but instead surrendered himself fully to God's plan. Even his own uncle had failed to notice the change in his nephew's looks and threw him

As told by a Franciscan writer of Saints, Marion A. Habig, O.F.M. (Order of Friars Minor):

*When he felt that his end was drawing near, Saint Roch asked that a priest might come and administer the last sacraments. The priest, on entering the prison, beheld it supernaturally lighted up and the poor captive surrounded with special radiance. As death claimed its victim, a tablet appeared on the wall on which an angelic hand wrote in golden letters the name of Roch, and the prediction that all who would invoke his intercession would be delivered from the plague. Informed of all that took place, Saint Roch's uncle came to the prison and, shortly after, also the governor's mother, that is, Roch's grandmother. She identified the dead man as her grandson by the birthmark of the red cross on his breast. They gave him a magnificent funeral and had a church built in his honour, in which his body was entombed. His veneration was approved by several popes and soon spread throughout Europe.* (illust. 56)

In 1414, during the Council of Constance, the plague returned to Rome. Prayers and public processions were performed in honour of Saint Roch, the patron saint of the plague, after which the disease disappeared. Saint Roch was a popular saint in the late Middle Ages, especially in the Italian towns where he practised his healing powers, and due to his patronage of infectious sickness, many of these communities have made him their benefactor.

This saint is commonly portrayed as a traveller with a walking staff and seashell (the sign of a pilgrim), often lifting his tunic to display the plague sore, or bubo, on his thigh, an angel by his side, and a dog carrying a loaf of bread in its mouth. He is the patron saint of dogs, dog owners, knee issues, surgeons, invalids, bachelors, diseased livestock, and against cholera, plague, skin rashes and infections, communicable diseases, pestilence, and epidemics.

## The Ghost of St Roch Cemetery

This cemetery was established in 1874 by the Rev. P. L. Thevis after the people of New Orleans prayed to Saint Roch, the patron saint of those seeking protection from epidemics, for help during a yellow fever outbreak. When none of the reverend's congregation perished from this disease, he promised to build a chapel in the cemetery in the saint's honour. (illust. 57)

The cemetery of Saint Roch is one of *the* largest cemeteries in New Orleans but it receives fewer visitors than its counterparts. No matter what hour of the day you visit you may find yourself...the only one there. Why? It's possible that a number of ghost stories originate from the Saint Roch Cemetery, which is famous for being haunted. Ghosts *do not* like to be disturbed. But, regardless of whether it is haunted or not, it is an ideal place to go, to unwind and take some time for yourself.

For more than a century, Saint Roch Cemetery has been the site of unexplained phenomena and reports of the supernatural. The ghost of a dog is said to roam the grounds. Yet the cemetery is not on the itinerary for any of the New Orleans Ghost Tours, which do not visit any residences in the French Quarter haunted by animals. (Although ghost tours offered in other cities, including Savannah, do.)

The urban legend surrounding the Saint Roch Cemetery Ghost Dog describes it as a monstrous black canine, and it is reported to have been captured on film as well as in pictures. There are rational people who wonder, 'Is it conceivable that it's only a stray dog walking the cemetery and not a ghost at all?' But some people have followed it about the cemetery, only to discover that it vanishes when cornered.

There are other accounts of supernatural occurrences in Saint Roch Cemetery, like the sightings of a person wearing a hood strolling the grounds when the gates are locked or passing through the cemetery walls. Is this mysterious hooded figure a ghost, or just an urban myth?

It is impossible to determine who this spirit is, but his clothes suggest he was once a member of the church. You never know, if you are able to visit Saint Roch Cemetery, you may get a glimpse of the ghostly form in a black cloak that to this day, wanders the grounds. (illust. 58)

# Foremost of the Westerners

by Bill Duvendack

## Anubis and Central America

Anubis, or Anpu, which is closer to his real name, has been thoroughly investigated and discussed in the context of the eastern hemisphere of the planet. He also has been discussed by various authors in the United States of America, but most of those writings look at his essence and, in a context, rooted there. It is generally common to find writings about him as he was in ancient Khem, and how it developed through Greek influence, as is the case with Hermanubis, but very little is discussed when it comes to Central and South America; a point which I would like to discuss here. Specifically, we will look at the connections and parallels between him and the Aztec god of death, Mictlantecuhtli, as well as Xolotl. (illust.59)

A great number of parallels between these three, shedding light on a piece of lost or forgotten history, and this is what we will be discussing here. I feel Anubis is clearly understood enough by now, so I will skip a lot of the preliminary background information about him and instead focus on the lesser-known Mictlantecuhtli and Xolotl. To know him, though, we must first take a cursory glance at history for context.

## Central America Pre-Aztec

Centuries after the classic period of the Mayan, a nomadic tribe came into Central America from what they referred to as Aztlan, or "The White Land," as it is known in their native tongue, Nahuatl. Immediately, their mysterious origins reveal themselves. This could be a reference to a variety of places that are reasonable to consider. This could be referring to northern Canada, particularly the areas that are snow and ice-covered for the majority of the year. Or, this could be a reference to the Salt Lake Desert in the northern part of the USA. It could also be a reference to the White Sands in the state of New Mexico in the USA. Or, liberally speaking, this could be a reference to northern Siberia.

Even though that seems like a stretch, in recent years, more and more information has been coming to light about the land bridge that used to stretch across the Bering Strait and the groups of people that came across it. Personally, it seems that this is a reference to the Salt Lake Desert, but ultimately this is all conjecture. Regardless of the truth of this is the fact that we immediately have an allusion to salt, which was a major component of Khemetic embalming procedures, giving us our first interesting point of consideration and connection. This group of hunters and gatherers were known as the "Aztecs," or alternately, 'Tenochca,' or 'Mexica.' 'Tenochca' was incorporated into the name of their capital city 'Tenochtitlan,' and their name of 'Mexica' became the root for the latter created Mexico City, and of course, became the name for the entire country in existence today.

## The Aztecs

Through political alliances and military conflict, they overthrew (or capitalized on the fall of) the ruling Toltecs of Central America in the early 13th century CE. Upon seeing an eagle on a cactus at lake Texcoco, the Aztecs decided to drain the swamp and establish their capital city, 'Tenochtitlan.' I find this a very interesting point because, in many ways, a swamp is a liminal space, and Anubis is associated with liminal spaces. To me, this shows a preternatural alignment between the two currents, rather than illustrating a connection, but it is worth noting, anyway.

Along with their thirst for conquest, they also brought their gods. Most of what we know about them came from the writings of the conquering Spaniards in the form of the Florentine Codex, recorded in the late 16th century by Friar Bernardino de Sahagun. Other codices have information as well but considering that around three hundred years had passed between the writing of that book and the arrival of the Aztecs, we can deduce that a lot had changed, gone missing, or been added. Then there's the fact that the friar was writing through a particularly religious-colored lens so that some material may be distorted. Something similar to this happened when Christian monks wrote about Norse stories. As is to be expected, a lot of these deities parallel those from other cultures, so we could easily invoke the law of correspondences and Jungian psychology to see various archetypes at play here, which were also in play in other parts of the planet during this time, as well as centuries prior.

There are generally thirteen categories of their gods, and each category contains at least five, but this number goes up substantially higher depending on the category. Breaking this down is beyond the scope of this essay, but it is another interesting point due to the parallel with ancient Khem centuries earlier, which had hundreds of deities. Like most ancient and classical civilizations, there were gods for many things, ranging from natural forces to medicine and commerce. Interestingly enough, they also had gods for the stars and abstract concepts such as excess and pleasure.

**Xolotl**
The first god to look at in the context of Anubis is the Aztec gold Xolotl. He was a god of fire and lightning, and while those two traits are not specifically Anubian, two of his other traits are. He was also known as a soul guide for the dead and was usually depicted as a dog-headed man. Other traits include being the god of twins, monsters, sickness, deformities, heavenly fire, and Venus in her evening star role, which aligns him with twilight, another liminal reference. In their mythology, he was the twin of Quetzalcoatl, the feathered serpent, who represented wisdom, Venus at dawn, the priesthood, and many other traits. Xolotl was

truly a darker god, in contrast to Quetzalcoatl, who was more aligned with the light. These two together reveal another subtle parallel between the Aztecs and ancient Egyptians-that of the role of Venus. While Egyptian astrotheology was focused around the star Sirius, Venus held the central position in Mesoamerica. Both Hathor and Isis have been said to correspond to Venus, and there is a growing amount of research that states that ancient Egyptians did travel this far across the ocean, specifically those that represented Isis. (illust. 60)

The obvious connections between Xolotl are present: soul guide for the dead, identifying with liminal places and times, and being a dog-headed human. However, through studying him, we can learn more about Anubis. Really, we do not know how old Anubis is, other than the fact he is one of the oldest gods of Egypt, dating back to predynastic times. While his first detailed introduction is in the Pyramid Texts, he had been around a long time before that. After all, it is commonly believed that those sacred texts were compiled over an extended period and are generally considered to be much, much older than the date that is usually ascribed to them. What this means is that there is probably much more lost information about Anubis than known information. It is that point we will turn our attention to now.

We know that Anubis was the original lord of the dead, and since all things die, it is safe to infer that he is the lord of many dead creatures that time has swallowed. Some of these could easily be seen as anonymous beasts and monsters by today's standards, and some of these could also be various biological human monstrosities too, such as would have included (in those times) people born with deformities. Part of the reason we arrive at that conclusion is that we know inbreeding was common in Egypt to keep the lineage pure, but many times, inbreeding leads to deformities, so it is not much of a stretch to equate Anubis with monsters in ancient Egypt, just like Xolotl in Mesoamerica.

Another interesting connection between Xolotl and ancient Egypt can be found regarding Set. In Aztec myth, Xolotl went out in front of the sun to protect it from dangers in the underworld in a manner very similar to Set's function with Ra. While this does not correspond with Anubis, it is worth mentioning because it shows yet another connection between ancient Egypt and the Aztec people. Another parallel between the two that spans all deities is that of human sacrifice. Both ancient Egyptians and Aztecs engaged in the practice, and while for very different reasons and techniques, it is still worth pointing out because it extends our list of parallels between the two cultures. The key to remember though is that there is approximately a 1500-year difference between the two. Classical ancient Egypt had fallen approximately 1500 years before the Aztecs rose to power.

Although we can clearly see strong connections between the two, we can also safely say that they did not exchange ideas. However, it is strongly possible and discussed in many places that the ancient Egyptians did make it to the western hemisphere during their times of glory, as is evidenced with the rune stone in Rune Stone State Park in the state of Oklahoma in the USA, various archaeological finds in the southwest of the USA, and strong parallels and connections between various pieces of Egyptian culture and the Mayans and Olmecs.

Coming back to Anubis, let us continue the parallels to the Aztec pantheon. Similar to ancient Egypt, dogs were sacrificed to be with their owners in the afterlife. Aztec culture's burial rites and procedures were not as extravagant or ritualistic as the ancient Egyptians, but this parallel is still highly interesting. Xolotl initially came from the southern part of Mesoamerica, which would have been where the Mayans dwelled centuries earlier. This fact more firmly cements the connection between the Mayans and ancient Egypt. A detail that bears mentioning is that in the Aztec calendar, the day associated with the dog is Mictlantecuhtli, the god of death and the ruler of the afterlife, known as Mictlan.

## Mictlantecutli

Xolotl and Mictlantecuhtli are not only connected through the calendrical correspondence mentioned above but also by the fact that both were many times depicted as skeletons. Specifically, both were depicted as skeletons at various states of decay, so you may find artwork for either of them that was very bloody and gory, with flesh, muscle, and blood dangling off the image. This was a much more visceral depiction of skeletons, whereas we may tend to think of them as being pristine skeletons.

He ruled the land of the dead and also all other death-related deities. The descriptions of him are quite graphic, such as the fact that he wore a necklace of human eyeballs. The skeletal image should be discussed briefly, though, as we find a much different interpretation than in other global cultures. (illust. 61)

In the Aztec culture, skeletons were viewed as symbols of fertility and abundance. Here, I am reminded of Egypt's black soil associated with fertility, rather than both black and skeletons being associated with decay and death in contemporary times. Cannibalism was also a common characteristic of his rituals, and through this, we can see the connection to human sacrifice. It was also said that during the daytime, his mouth would swallow the stars.

Like ancient Egypt, the dead were often buried with belongings and things they might need in the afterlife. Eventually, they would be given to Mictlantecutli as tribute. Mictlantecutli presided over this, too, and helped the souls along to wherever they might go. There were various levels of the underworld in Aztec cosmology, so part of his duties was psychopomp in nature. Besides ushering souls to those various places, he would also bring souls into babies born on the calendar day that he ruled. By looking at Mictlantecutli and Xolotl, we get a look at two aspects of Anubis that are generally not considered in conventional and orthodox thinking. Anubis was the lord of the dead, but what did that mean? Were the deceased to give tribute to him from the stores of what they were buried with? Was cannibalism something that was practiced at some of his sacred sites? Cannibalism is, after all, a very visceral rite of showing the connection between life and death and is very reminiscent of another ancient Egyptian symbol, the ouroboros.

**Closing Remarks**
As you can see, in true pathfinder fashion, we began this piece with Anubis as our guide and ended up cursory exploring the connection between ancient Egypt and Central America. Even though the Aztecs and their empire arose centuries after the fall of Egypt, it appears that there were images, traditions, and other parallels that continued from the time of contact between the Egyptians and the Olmecs and Mayans. The timeline would thus be contact between Egypt, first with the Olmecs and then with the Mayans. But, we should be careful not to think too linearly about this, as they most likely dealt with the Olmecs and Mayans simultaneously. Since there are more parallels between the Mayans and the Egyptians rather than the Olmecs and the Egyptians, it seems that was their primary connection.

We should also discuss how this contact took place. Conventional thought says that Egyptians went through the Mediterranean into the Atlantic and then on to the western hemisphere from there, but it is just as, if not more, plausible that they went east, going through the Pacific to reach Mesoamerica. This is due to the work of the Kon-Tiki expedition by Thor Heyerdahl in 1947, which proved that this route did happen. Most of the discussion about Egyptians coming across the Atlantic hinges on the thought that in the Atlantic Ocean, beyond the Strait of Gibraltar, there was once a landmass that would have been the destination or at least a resting point for them as they traveled. However, unlike Thor Heyerdahl's work, there is no proof to support this theory. This does not mean that it didn't happen, but rather the more plausible route would have been across the Pacific Ocean, the larger of the two. Regardless, it is an interesting situation to consider because either way proves that ancient Egyptians were potentially and probably the first people to reach the western hemisphere.

Coming with them were their Neters, their gods, and even though the Egyptian empire fell, the impact of their gods on indigenous people in Central America remained and evolved, their practices and beliefs becoming synthesized with what was happening there. Most of the study of this has been on the outskirts of conventional academic research and schools of thought, but we can see that while that might be true now, it will most likely change in the future. By studying the Aztec and Mayan mythologies and pantheons, we can learn more about ancient Egypt.

To this day, Anubis cults still exist in Mexico, but this information is not easily found or readily available. I have only recently learned about this from Mexicans, who spoke of oral traditions and legends in their home areas. These cults are similar to the Santa Muerte cults common in society and cartels, except that they are more in line with Xolotl when it comes to symbolism and imagery. I see this as a direct descendant of what we have been discussing here, and it is proof positive that when an impact is made on culture and society, the effects never really go away; they adapt and persevere.

## Bibliography
Budge, E.A. Wallis., The Gods of the Egyptians 1 & 2, Dover Publications, 1969
Bunson, Margaret., The Encyclopedia of Ancient Egypt, Gramercy Books, 1991
Butler, Edward P., *Goddesses and Gods of the Ancient Egyptians*, Phaidra Editions, 2021
Carabas, Markus., *Anubis*, Charles River Editors, 2018

Clark, Rosemary., *The Sacred Magic of Ancient Egypt*, Llewellyn Publications, 2008

Clark, Rosemary., *The Sacred Tradition in Ancient Egypt*, Llewellyn Publications, 2008

DuQuesne, Terence., *Jackal at the Shaman's Gate*, Darengo, 1991

Page, Judith, and Jan A Malique., *Pathworking with the Egyptian Gods*, Llewellyn Publishing, 2007

Page, Judith, and Ken Biles., *Invoking the Egyptian Gods*, Llewellyn Publishing, 2012

# Black Dogs in Folklore

### by Bob Trubshaw

*For he was speechless, ghastly, wan,*
*Like him of whom the story ran,*
*Who spoke the spectre hound in man.*

Sir Walter Scott,
*The lay of the last minstrel,* Canto VI, v.26.

Why is the death-hound of Arthur Conan Doyle's *The Hound of the Baskervilles* such a vigorous archetypal beast? Conan Doyle's inspiration was the folk tale of a phantom black dog on Dartmoor. Such beasts recur throughout Britain, with almost every county having at least one example. A typical reference appears in the Rev Worthington-Smith's book on the folklore of Dunstable, published in 1910: 
*'Another belief is that there are ghostly black dogs, the size of large retrievers, about the fields at night, that these dogs are generally near gates and stiles, and are of such a forbidding aspect that no one dares venture to pass them and that it means death to shout at them. In some places, the spectral dog is named "Shuck" and is said to be headless.'* [1] (illust.62)

It is interesting that Worthington-Smith refers to the name 'Shuck'. I doubt that this is a name normally used in Dunstable, as this is normally associated with Norfolk, where the reference is more typically to 'Old Shuck'.

In Suffolk the black dog becomes 'Old Shock' (both these probably derive from the Old English *scucca*, meaning 'demon').

In the Quantock Hills of Somerset, the black dog was frequently seen and called the 'Gurt Dog'. Cornwall has various tales of the 'Devil's Dandy (or Dando) Dogs', Devon has the 'Yeth (Heath) or Wisht Hounds. Other local names include Barguest, Black Shag, Padfoot, or Hooter. Just to be different, in West Yorkshire the common name is 'Guytrash'; in Lancashire, this is reduced to 'Trash' or changed to 'Skriker'. Further afield, a particularly unpleasant phantom pooch frequented Peel Castle on the Isle of Man in the seventeenth century and was known as the Moddey Dhoo, or Mauthe Doog. In Ireland, we hear of the Pooka. (illust. 63)

Although Theo Brown produced a detailed and useful survey of black dog lore in a *Folklore* article in 1958, [2] she went on to collect considerably more material but was unable to collate it into publishable form by the time of her death last year [3].

In the Mercian area there are at least seven examples for Warwickshire alone:

*At Alveston, Charles Walton, a plowboy, met a phantom black dog on his way home on nine successive evenings. On the final occasion a headless lady in a silk gown rushed past him, and the following day he heard of his sister's death.* [4]

The apparition of a tall lady with a large black dog at her side has been seen at Pickerings Barn in Brailes. [5]

During the Second World War at Brook House, Snitterfield (which used to be the Bell Brook Inn) a big black dog was seen. It ran over the tilled earth of the garden without leaving footprints. [6] Very old people of Warwick used to say that the castle was haunted by a black dog. The tale has the hallmarks of a time-encrusted tall story. The local version claims it all started when an old retainer there, a woman called Moll Bloxham, sold milk and butter from the castle stores for her personal gain. One Christmas she overdid this, and the then Earl of Warwick, getting wind of it, stopped her source of supply. Furiously angry, she vowed she would 'get them haunted'. She apparently succeeded and returned in the form of a big black dog. In due course, the clergy was called in to exorcise the ghost with a bell, book, and candle, but for a time they were entirely unsuccessful. Then one day, so it was said, a huge black dog sprang from Caesar's Tower into the river below, and so ended the ghost story. [7] (illust. 64)

A black dog with a matted, shaggy coat and green eyes roams in Whitmore Park at night. Local people avoided the area since seeing the dog means a death in the family [8].

Meon Hill has both a phantom black dog and a ghostly pack of white hounds. The death of George Walton in very curious circumstances on 14th February 1945 was accompanied by a black dog being hung in a nearby tree. Walton had seen a black dog on nine occasions - the last time it changed into a headless black woman. His sister died shortly after. Although strongly contested, Walton's death has many overtones of the ritual sacrifice of a 'cunning man'.

In Nottinghamshire, only one black dog story is known. A manuscript dating to 1952 in Nottingham County Library records the words of Mrs. Smalley who was then about 75 years old. 'Her grandfather, who was born in 1804 and died in 1888, used to have occasion to drive from Southwell to Bathley [near South Muskham] in a pony and trap. This involved going along Crow Lane, which leaves South Muskham opposite the school and goes to Bathley. Frequently, along that lane, he saw a black dog trotting alongside his trap. Around about 1915 his great-grandson, Mrs. Smalley's son Sidney, used to ride out from Newark on a motorcycle to their home at Bathley. He went into Newark to dances and frequently returned at about 11 o'clock at night. He too often saw a black dog in Crow lane; he sometimes tried to run over it but was never able to. One night Sidney took his father on the back of the motorcycle especially to see the dog, and both of them saw it.' [9]

Moving across to Lincolnshire there are a number of examples. The two best-known appear in Ethel Rudkin's book [10]. 'The road up to Moortown House was haunted by a big black dog that always disappeared into the hedge at the same place.' And at Blyborough 'The Black Dog has been seen near the Fish Pond and near the 'Old Yard'. However, Rudkin's 1938 article in *Folklore* [11] lists a much greater number - by 1958 there were 47 separate black dog localities in Lincolnshire [12].

In 1127 a rapacious Abbot called Henry of Poitou was appointed to Peterborough Abbey. The chronicler of the day records 'tat as soon as he came there . . . the soon afterward many people saw and heard many hunters hunting. The hunters were black and big and loathsome, and their hounds all black and wide-eyed and loathsome, and they rode on black horses and black goats.' Such a wild hunt was reported at a similar time in the Welsh Marches by Walter Map, written about 1190. Walter's map also gave us the legend of Wild Edric in the Clun area of the Marches. As late as last century Edric was said to haunt the hills around Church Stretton - in the form of a huge black dog. [13] (illust. 65)

Such packs of spectral hounds - with or without hunters - have been seen all over Europe and are generally known as the Gabriel Hounds or Gabble Retchets in Britain, and as the Wild Hunt in Germany and Woden's Hunt in Scandinavia. They are similar to the Seven Whistlers in that they were a portent of death or disaster. Perhaps the association with Gabriel and an old word for 'corpse'.

Clearly, these wild hunts are also like the Welsh tales of Cwm Annwn, the spectral hunt, and even the Wandering Jew folklore which is known throughout Europe. To what extent all these sky-traversing hounds are the last vestiges of a complex and ancient cosmological mythology is a matter of academic debate.

I will just observe here that as far away as the New World the Cherokee Indians refer to the Milky Way as 'Where the dog ran'. A dog that ran from a corn mill in the south towards the north, dropping meal as he ran, is given as the origin of the Milky Way in Scandinavian legends too. [14]

I know of no examples of phantom black dogs in Leicestershire and Rutland and only circumstantial accounts of one at Retford, Nottinghamshire.

Although a country-wide survey would extend well beyond the confines of this article - indeed beyond the whole issue of *Mercian*

*Mysteries* - I will venture to mention two examples from West Yorkshire which might not be more widely known.

In Thornton, near Bradford, Jim Craven Well (104:SE1033) was the haunt of the ghost of 'Peggy wi't Lantern' and 'Bloody Tongue', a great dog with red eyes and a huge tail. The well is now lost [15].

A spectral hound with large glowing red eyes traditionally haunts Helliwell Banks Well, Baildon (104:16103962; now capped over), and the nearby Slaughter Lane. Several other wells in West Yorkshire are associated with the 'Guytrash' which takes the form of a large shaggy dog with broad webbed feet. It has drooping 'saucer' eyes and walks with a splashing sound (the 'trash' sound of old-fashioned boots) [16]

Folklore also tells us of some dramatic consequences resulting from the sighting of black dogs.

Somerset has a black dog that appeared in 1960 to two people - who both died soon after. East Anglia, Essex, and Buckinghamshire all have examples of phantom dogs which disappeared in dramatic flashes, in one case burning to death a farmer, his horse, and wagon. (illust.66)

On Sunday 4th August 1577 an extremely violent thunderstorm shook the church of Bungay, Suffolk. A fearful-looking black dog appeared inside the church, in front of the parishioners. Two who were touched by the animal were instantly killed and a third shriveled up like a drawn purse. On the same day, a similar hound appeared in the church at Blythburgh, seven miles away, also killing three people and 'blasting' others. The market's weathervane depicts the fiendish hound. Other such devastating apparitions had been recorded, for some time before 1613, a bull-like creature manifested inside the church at Great Chart in Kent, leaving a trail of dead and seriously injured, before demolishing a part of a wall and disappearing. [17; 18]

As a link to my article elsewhere in this issue on the mythology of dogs, I will draw upon just a few examples most relevant to Earth mysteries. In Wiltshire, Bishops Canning has a black dog legend associated with a stile into the churchyard and a possible ley - and 40 or so other black dogs are also recorded for that county alone [19].

Theo Brown states bluntly: 'Roads. These seem to be the natural home of Black Dogs. I have at least 55 examples of these . . . In addition to the above, there are nine haunting bridges. Numerically it looks as though the emphasis is on the man-made road being guarded, rather than the natural stream.' [20]

Other writers have speculated on the links between these phantom black dogs and leys. Janet and Colin Bord, in a chapter of *Alien animals* giving a comprehensive account of phantom dogs, show that a number of such sightings occur in places - such as churchyards and barrows - which are Watkins-style 'ley markers' and have a list of four tentative alignments in Lincolnshire which are associated with black dog sightings (Algakirk; Northorpe; North Kelsey; Blyborough) [21].

## Acknowledgements
I am indebted to a number of friends for responding to my request for information on phantom black dog legends; in particular Jeremy Harte and also Pat Bradford, Janet Bord, Bob Dickinson, Frank Earp, and John Michell.

## References
1: Rev Worthington-Smith, *Dunstable and its surrounds*, 1910.
2: Theo Brown, 'The black dog', *Folklore*, Sept 1958 p175-192.
3: Her notes are now deposited with the University of Exeter library. I can only hope that sooner rather than later a post-graduate student obtains funding to compile these into a publishable book.
4: Roy Palmer, *The folklore of Warwickshire*, Batsford, 1976.
5: Alfred Woodward, *Memories of Brailes*, Peter Drinkwater, 1988.
6: Palmer, *op. cit.*
7: David Green, *A Warwickshire Christmas*, Alan Sutton, 1980.

8: Palmer, *op. cit.*
9: Nottingham County Library MS; information kindly supplied by Frank Earp.
10: Ethel H. Rudkin, *Lincolnshire folklore*, Beltons, 1936.
11: Ethel H. Rudkin, 'The black dog', *Folklore*, June 1938, p111-113
12: Brown, *op. cit.*
13: Jennifer Westwood, *Albion - a guide to legendary Britain*, Granada, 1985
14: G. de Santillana and H. von Dechend, *Hamlet's mill* Macmillan 1970
15: Val Shepherd, *Historic wells in and around Bradford*, Heart of Albion Press, 1994; citing T. Mackenzie, *Bronte moors and villages*, 1923.
16: Shepherd, *op. cit.*
17: John Michell and Bob Rickard, *Phenomena: a book of wonders*, Thames and Hudson 1977.
18: Westwood, *op. cit.*
19: John Michell, *Earthspirit*, Thames and Hudson, 1975; citing Kathleen Wiltshire, *Ghosts and legends of the Wiltshire countryside*, Salisbury, 1973.
20: Brown, *op. cit.*
21: Janet and Colin Bord, *Alien animals*, Panther, 2nd ed 1985.

**Black dogs - stop press latest**
Just when I thought I'd got to grips with just about everything worthwhile on the subject, up barks Peter Jennings's article on Black Shuck legends in the latest *Gippeswic* [1].

In addition to some more examples of black dog apparitions in East Anglia, two very interesting ideas emerge from this survey. Jennings notes that black dog sightings seem to be especially prevalent in East Anglia and the Yorkshire east coast - areas that were heavily settled by Scandinavians from the seventh century. A link with Norse traditions does, of course, fit in well with the mythology discussed by Alby Stone and myself in our articles. Personally, I would want to make a more accurate assessment of the distribution before making such an assertion - there are, after all, many examples too from other regions and counties with plenty of recorded examples of black dogs are usually simply those where a folklorist has been particularly active.

One other snippet of speculation more strongly suggests Scandinavian associations. As I have noted, black dogs appear under a variety of regional names. One such is 'barguest', prevalent in parts of Yorkshire. Peter Jennings reports that Sir Walter Scott suggested that this appellation came from the German *bargeist*, 'spirit of the (funeral) bier'. Now that really does fit in exceptionally well with the 'guardian of the corpse ways' concept. Many thanks, Peter, for drawing attention to this - even if you would prefer to see the origin as implying some sort of guardian spirit who 'bars' unwanted 'guests' (though, that too, has strongly liminal associations). (illust. 67)

On a lighter note, Jennings informs us that in Suffolk there is a Black Shuck Borderline Morris team. Is the 'borderline' aspect merely an unconscious affirmation of the liminal role of the Shuck mythos?
1: *Gippeswic* No.9, June 1994, GBP1.75 from 42 Cemetery Road, Ipswich, IP4 2JA
Originally published in *Mercian Mysteri* No.20 August 1994.

## Anubis: A story of ancient Egypt

**by Michael Starsheen**

Anubis sat in the dry, desert air on the cliffs above the West Bank of the Nile, deep in thought. It was the end of the season of Shomu and the Epagomenal Days were passing, and he was waiting for a sign. The dark night was still and serene; most everyone was asleep. He kept his watch toward the East.

The night began to brighten, and birds began to sing softly as dawn approached. Anubis watched the horizon carefully, and finally, there it was! The bright, blue star, Sopdet, Star of Isis appeared briefly on the horizon, only to be lost in the glare of sunlight as Ra-Harakte rose on the last of the Epagomenal Days.

He knew that it was the signal for the Nile to rise, as it had every year for millennia. He shifted his attention to the isle of Elephantine, where Hapi guarded the sacred caves from which the flood would come. (illust. 68)

At first, there was a trickle, as Hapi opened the gates of the South, then gradually the flow strengthened and quickened. He could see the green vegetation caught in the flow and knew it as the pieces of Osiris' body, Set had hacked into pieces during the Harvest. He began to help Isis and Nephthys collect the pieces and set up a mortuary tent at el-Qeis to begin the task of embalming them. Gradually, as the flow of the Nile continued to strengthen, the three gods gathered the 14 parts of Osiris' body they could find, as the floodwaters touched the places in Khemet where they had been hidden.

The flood revealed Set's caches, and so it went. As each piece was recovered, Anubis mummified it and placed it with the others in the proper configuration for Osiris' body.

The flow shifted from the green vegetation to the red soil from upstream representing the blood of Osiris. This they also gathered in, to help refresh and revivify Osiris' body. Isis and Nephthys watched as Anubis reassembled Osiris' body to its original form and began the spells that would bring him back to life. (illust. 69)

Isis opined that she could not find Osiris' phallus anywhere! Nephthys replied that she couldn't either. So, Anubis suggested that Isis make a phallus to replace the lost one, and she began to carve one from the wood of the Persea tree, which was sacred to Osiris. When it was done, Anubis incorporated it into the corpse and began reciting the spells to reanimate the body, along with Isis and Nephthys.

For 70 days, they chanted over the body, as the flood rose and fell, and the land received its bounty of new soil for the new year. Osiris' body was complete, but still, he was not reanimated. Isis and Nephthys fanned him with their wings to give Osiris breath again, but the process was continuing as the seasons shifted from Akhet to Peret. Gradually, the spells and the breath began to bring Osiris around, until the grain began to sprout again from his sacred form. In this way, the gods knew their work had been successful; Osiris was renewed and reborn.

Isis coupled with Osiris and became pregnant with the divine Horus, once more the land of Khemet became fertile and filled with growing grain again. The tiny shoots were cared for tenderly, at first, because the Osiris was still weak from his ordeal, but as the grain grew and became tall, he increased in vigor. Isis and Nephthys were delighted with his recovery and stood by his side as he watched the land grow green, and then golden.

Peret passed into the season of Shomu once again, when the grain was high, and the Black Land shone golden with ripe wheat and barley. It was time for Anubis to open the way to the Underworld, where Osiris would rule the harvest of life. As all the gods gathered in the Halls of Ma'at, Osiris took his throne with Isis and Nephthys standing behind, sheltering him with their wings.

Anubis began to lead the people who had passed away, to stand before Osiris for Judgment. Anubis stood by the balance as hearts were weighed against the feather of Ma'at, carefully adjusting the measure until the heart was proven true — or not. Those who were seen to be true of heart, and justified, Anubis guided from the hall and through the remainder of the Duat to the gates of the North. There, he helped them to rise to the Imperishable Stars of their destiny; to live forever in the Field of Reeds.

For those who were not balanced, Anubis gave to the demon, Ammit, who eagerly devoured them, casting the poor souls back into incarnation to try again. They would rise as Osiris did each flood season and find their way back to the halls of Ma'at, and the cycle would continue. Once more, Anubis waited upon his mountain, in the chill, dry dark, watching for Sirius to rise and signal the New Year was beginning again.

So mote it be

**Bibliography**

Assman, J., *The Mind of Egypt*: History and meaning in the time of the pharaohs, New York, NY: Henry Holt and Company. 1996

Budge, E.A. Wallis, *The Gods of the Egyptians*: Studies in Egyptian Mythology. New York, NY: Dover Publications 1969

Budge, E.A. Wallis, *Osiris & the Egyptian Resurrection*. New York, NY: Dover Publications 197

Faulkner, R. O., *The Ancient Egyptian Coffin Texts*. Oxford, UK: Aris and Philips, 1973

Faulkner, R. O., *The Ancient Egyptian Pyramid Texts*. New York, NY: Oxford University Press, 1969

Pinch, G., *Egyptian Mythology*: A guide to the gods, goddesses, & traditions of ancient Egypt. New York, NY: Oxford University Press, 2002

Wilkinson, R. H., *The Complete Gods and Goddesses of Ancient Egypt*. London, UK: Thames & Hudson, 2003

# Ritual of Descent

### by Dr. Tim Broussard

Being a Visionary
An Account of Initiation into Anubis Gnosticism

### The Grey Gate of Life

Rising from the floor of the wasteland, I beheld a pyramid gleaming in the setting Sun, of seven steps rising toward the stars and the realms of those stars and them that dwell within. But hark, what is found at the base of the pyramid? A door of grey metal, and upon the door is written in white the word DEATH. No longer did I yearn for the stars of the sky, but rather did I cast off my fears, and seek to know with the living mind what lay beyond the door of death.

As I lay my hand upon the door to make my way inside, a voice came forth from the Sun, even as it was falling, imploring me to ascend and be one with the Gods, lest I be forsaken and forgotten, a shadow to the world. Fears once more assailed, but another voice arose to drown out the voice of the light and the fears born of living in the light. This voice came not from without but from within, as though the voice was in my very blood. It said, 'Death and life, to know one, is to know the other. Embrace life and in time you shall know death. Embrace death and you shall know life, and time shall be but a road of choice.'

My hand upon the door burned as the words of the voice of the blood became as coal in my hand; at that moment, a choice made, I pressed through my pain and found the door did not open, but rather I passed through into what appeared to be a tomb. I turned and looked from whence I had come and found upon a white door of ivory in the colour of amber was written LIFE.

I looked to my person and found I was bare to the waist and, all about me, ash, as though from a great fire, floated in the air. Where the treasure should have been if indeed this was a tomb, there were skulls, and where the sarcophagus should have been was a hole or pit, and emitted therefrom a sweetness, as of gardens mingled with bitterness and musk, as of deer fleshly slain. As my eyes adjusted to the gloom, they found emerald light faintly coming from the eyes of the many skulls. Heat and fear called forth sweat from my body and the ash clung thereto, coating my form in the remains of what must have been an inner fire. Recalling my choice, there was naught to do but go on, for I knew I had forsaken the path of union for the path of isolation.

**Step One:**
I looked into the pit, past the fumes which flowed upward, and found a step as of polished silver, and I stepped thereupon. From the silver step, I looked up and found, not the roof of the chamber, but rather, the night sky and, in that sky, stars strung on lines of violet fire on the velvet of the night.

As I looked, the air grew cold and in that cold was the exit of both past and future; what had been, was no more and so was its future, and I knew this to be freedom, to be utterly alone. Tears fell till they ran down my body and collected in my hands. Those in my left hand became a chalice and those in my right became a blade. I looked ahead of me and the gloom lifted, and my eyes further grew at ease in the dark. I saw that I stood in a hall and on the walls were carved the scenes of my life, going backward from when I had approached the door.

As I moved down the hall, I saw, what had been my life around me. At the end of the hall rose a stone altar, on which I rested the chalice and the blade. There was a cry, as of a child, and there was upon the altar what had been me as a child.

The voice of my blood and its fire rose from within my chest, and the voice said, 'Sever your mortal bonds, slay what was and could have been.' The fires within pained me and with the blade, I opened the throat of the child that had been and now never was. 'It's blood,' the voice said, 'take this blood for your wine.' and so I did. The blood's warmth flooded me and when I looked at the altar it was gone and another step down was in its place.

**Step Two:**
The step down had the sheen of blood upon it and, in taking it, I found myself in a river of human blood and I could but travel by its current. The voice of my own blood spoke and revealed this as the blood of the lost, the blood of those who will neither ascend nor descend. Now, did I understand, that this was not the same as my blood; my blood burned and spoke with a fire. I was filled with thirst and did drink; by this was the fire in my blood ignited.

I drank, and in drinking, knew that to drink the blood of the lost is to be the hunter of the lost, and in so being, reclaim life. The river carried me to a bank of iron which led to a platform of the same. The air, as before, was cold, but the blood from the river warmed me, from within and without.

On the platform was inscribed the image of the boat of Ra, but in the place of Ra, Seker stood. Before me, appeared Anubis, who said to me, 'To Man and his world I am the guide of the Dead and the judge of souls. To thee and those who do as thou hast done, I am the Son of Set and his voice, for those like thee who are born of the blood of his mouth as it falls as He devours the lost.' As the echoes of the words of Anubis faded, violet fire issued forth from his mouth and entered my mouth and when my vision cleared, Anubis was gone and in his place on the floor was an aperture.

**Step Three:**
I looked into the aperture and found a third step, which radiated with the colour violet. I descended the step and found myself in the midst of a great storm, and in looking up, saw that I stood on dry land under an ocean of blood. Looking up at the storm, I saw its beauty and the patterns those caught in the storm will never see. In joy, from my heart, praise erupted, and my voice rang forth, rising

into the storm from below, as thunder. With the release of praise, I felt a fire alight in my heart and the flame grow, until my very heart was consumed, so that this violet fire filled my eyes and burst forth from my chest, consuming the ash and dried blood of my passage.

The whole of my form was ablaze with violet fire, and in the silence of my ecstasy, I knew this fire to be the force of my will. The fire receded into the hollow where my mortal heart had been and, in the place of my heart, was a stone of hæmatite, and the voice of my blood spoke, saying, 'Behold the Seed of the treasure of the wise, the pale bloodstone that liberates the will!' The fire had passed, and I beheld that the form that had been mine was no more, and in its place was a humanoid being with scales the colour of dried blood, and about my shoulders was a hooded mantle of black, on which were runes and signs in violet, red, and silver. Belted at my waist was a sword and, when I drew it, the blade gleamed violet, and I knew I looked upon my will made manifest. I made my way across the land I stood upon and, upon hearing a sound behind me, I turned and saw that where I had stepped, grew lotus flowers. From the storm that raged above fell a bolt of lightning struck the sand before my feet, opening the ground and leaving in its wake a pile of diamonds on either side of the hole. Sheathing my sword and trusting in my will, I stepped into the hole.

**Step Four:**
My feet found purchase on a step of black onyx, and I found myself in a white room. In the centre of this room was a pool of liquid the colour of emerald that smelled of Wormwood. On the surface of the pool burned a Black Flame that rose to the ceiling; out of the flame stepped forth Anubis, who raised his hand in benediction. At the Blessing of the God, there appeared on the floor piles of bones. On the foreheads of the skulls were carved runes that spelled the names of kings, and Anubis's voice roared in my blood saying, 'Burn now the bones and invigorate thy spirit, claim the power of them who were kings in life!' I gathered in my arms the bones of the Dead and cast them into the fiery pool. In the Black Flame burned the bones and, as they burned, I saw the sparks of violet fire. Silently, knowing, I reached into the folds of my mantle and brought forth the chalice. I dipped the chalice in the pool and saw

the embers gather therein and, raising a toast to the honour of the Dead; I drank and knew my powers had been increased.

Anubis again spoke, 'See you now the irony of death, of the fear it calls forth? That which remains of the Dead becomes the foundation for the future.' At the end of his words did the dreaded god disintegrate into powered hæmatite before my very eyes. I walked around the pool until I stood where the god had been and found that where the room had been, was no more. I stood in a field of salt, and where the pool had been, a broken jackal's skull rested upon a door. Around my feet still, the hæmatite powder still lay. Using the cap of the skull as a bowl, I gathered the powder, and a great wind came and pulled the door free.

**Step Five**:
Escaping the wind, I descended and found I stood upon a golden step. Before me was revealed a room of many pillars and against one wall was raised an altar of wood and granite, on which rested two candles, one black, and the other gold. On the floor before the altar was the image of the scales of judgment overturned and the ape of Thoth slain. I went before the altar and closing my eyes, sought my power for guidance. In response rose the voice of my blood, saying, 'For power was guidance sacrificed, and yet is nothing lost. Exchange fullness for hunger and make a potion as pale as water, spiced with the tears of the Dead.'

From my mantle, I drew the blade that came with the chalice, with my right hand I opened the veins of my left wrist. In the bowl of bone, I mixed the powdered hæmatite with my own blood. Then spake the voice of my blood, 'Cast thy medicine upon the altar of REASON that it be cured and the madness of EXPERIENCE be born.' I cast the chalice and what it contained upon the stone and the chalice was shattered, causing a shower that went from red and grey to gold.

I looked about marvelling at the act of transmutation and where the pillars had been, were scrolls and books. The cloud of gold coalesced before me and Anubis stood, arrayed in robes of red, green, and black, girt with a sword like my own. In his left hand, the god held a lamp in the shape of an hourglass, and in his right, a staff of polished bone. He bade me smear the remains from the bowl upon my blade and to strike the altar. I smeared the blade as the god asked, but my blade became heavy in my hands. Anubis spoke, 'Here is thy ignorance.' Rage filled my heart. Had I not gone on, in spite of the gods? Had I not sacrificed past and future for an eternal present?

My rage turned as cold as the air at dawn, and in that cold, I found my strength. I raised my blade as though it was a feather and smote the stone. It did shatter and was consumed by beetles that rose from where the stone had been. The beetles swarmed upon each other and did form a Throne, on the seat of which was a Black Book with red pages. Anubis bade me assume the Throne and after I did Anubis brought to me ink and for pen, the feather of Ma'at. He brought me the scrolls and books, and for Æons of Man's time did I learn, and after learning, did I practice. I filled my book with what I knew to be true from use until Anubis's hourglass dimmed, and I looked up to find myself alone and the lamp went black.

I could see no door or passage and so I went to my book for the answer. I found not my book but that card which bears the name TOWER and the legend THIS PLACE IS TERRIBLE. My inner fire rose, and the card burned as an amulet might, and out of the smoke a door formed, hanging slightly off the floor. I stood upon the seat of the Throne and leaped through the ephemeral passage.

**Step Six:**
I stood on a scorched field on which were traced the signs of the Zodiac, and in the centre, an opening surrounded by poles, on which eagles were impaled. I stepped from the platform and saw that it was a pyramid of emeralds. Knights in white upon red horses rode up to where I stood and charged me with the murder of Osiris and the debauching of Isis. I drew my blade and out of my mouth came the voice of Anubis, 'The law and the pretense of piety are ground up for the ink of the book of the Dead. Those who seek the release to fly shall be forever bound as those who never act out of regret for sins never committed shall be forever damned.' From my mouth flew a golden bird that struck the knights and turned them

to glass, which I shattered with my sword. Splinters of glass fell to the earth, which became an emerald stream that flowed into the opening. I knelt by the stream and brought its water to my lips and knew that this was the blood of my true Fathers. The eagle's scream broke my thoughts and I looked to find that the poles had become pillars, one of gold and the other of black onyx.

On the black, in emerald, was written power and on the gold was written, in emerald, knowledge. The signs of the stars began to burn, and music filled the air, the wound on my wrist began to burn and I looked and saw green tears of blood at the edges of a fading scar that was being replaced by a raised tattoo. The mark was that of an eclipse and I heard in my heart, 'Rest not, want always, desire, need, rage and rend!' I waded in the stream that I knew to be the blood of my ancestors, toward the opening, as the field burned. At last, I reached the opening and got out of the stream, finding that I stood in a chamber of crimson brick and the opening was a portal of stained glass that bore the sign of the Oroborus.

**Step Seven:**
Above the portal, I made the Sign of Anubis and spoke the words of the entrance. The portal opened outward and into it, I stepped; looking down I saw that I stood on a step of platinum, and looking behind me found the portal gone, and above me a night sky, but not the stars of Earth. Ahead of me, I saw a path defined by torches of white fire leading to a black pyramid of seven steps, at the top of which two golden serpents embraced. I drew my blade, sensing the need for it and in my hand, it became a staff carved as a serpent with the head of a wolf. I moved to walk and as my staff smote the ground, violet runes flared along with my steps. As I walked, the way became darker, and it seemed the stars were brighter and perhaps closer. The white torches became as motes of dust in the air, and the flash of the runes, the sheen of the stars upon the designs of my mantle. The distance ceased to be, and I stood before the pyramid. Upon the door to the pyramid is the sign of the Oroborus and from its centre was an eight-rayed star, in the centre of the star was an open eye. I do not call on my fire; I have become the fire that was once mine. As fire, I pass through the stones whose mortar is the blood of the lost and the satisfied. Flame becomes flesh

and ash becomes the mantle once more. With eyes, I looked upon the chamber where I found myself and saw upon the walls were carved the words:

*IN EMPTINESS ALONE IS ILLUMINATION, SO MUCH MORE IS WON BY FORSAKING THE LIFE AND LIGHT WITHOUT AND EMBRACING THE SPARK WITHIN BY PLUNGING INTO THE MAZE OF SELF AND THE ECSTASY OF NEED!*

## The Lapis Gate of Eternity

I read the words aloud and knew the truth of them and in that truth, I had the kiss of peace; around me on a floor of platinum, emerald, and gold were scattered the parts of both Osiris' and Apep's corpses. Thoth and his ape are given up to fornication. Isis debauched kneels, robed in scarlet, as Astarte the faithful wife of Sutekh demands service from her maiden slave. As my feet touch stone with the warmth of living flesh, I take a step and crush the skull of Ptah. Chained to his overturned Throne, Ra can but glare with blinded eyes and curse in silence with Tongue of Ash. I come to an altar on which Horus, drunk on the passion of his Father, reclines. At the head and foot of Horus are the red and the white crowns of the two lands, at each side of the altar priests stand ready to crown me if I so choose.

In each hand, I take up a crown and turn to face the gods in the chamber. 'I in life have taken the road of death and in the void found the radiance of darkness; I have descended into the funerary mountain and found the gold of knowledge and the onyx of power.' At the climax of my declaration, I smashed the crowns of the two lands, and with the powder of each, I turn to face, to look upon feeble Horus. I mingle the powders upon his papyrus skin, and it begins to burn before his phallus is consumed. with claws, I tear it free. I turn as the altar burns and press the phallus to the lips of the betrayer of my Father. As this is done a gate of Lapis appears and carved thereupon is the sign of DEATH. Fire from the altar pours toward the corpses on the floor, and as the smoke fills the chamber, Sutekh my Father rises from beneath the flames. Says the God onto me, 'Kneel not unto me for I am but a shadow of thy future, and thou art but a ghost of my past.' He formed from the

smoke and fire of the chamber a halo of darkest radiance.
Spoke again did He my Father, 'Thou art me crowned with eternity, Set-Heh: Darkness eternal!' He finished speaking and merged with the smoke and fire, all that was not me was by flame consumed, and at end, do only I, and the gate of Lapis remain. In the void I speak unto the gate, 'I have united all in nothing, I have naught but the present eternal, for me the gate shall open!' The gate opened and I stepped through. Behold is worked the great reversal, that gate which at the centre of the universe opens not onto the depth but the heights.

From my back spread wings of scale and leather. I, who have passed through the worlds below, return from above, in the robes of the stars, crowned with eternity, have come forth by night! Behind me, the black pyramid burned, and from its ruins, Seker rises not as the falcon but as the black hawk. The star entombed by day has risen, freed is eternity, Sutekh-Seker has assumed his Throne in the Underworld. On Earth is beheld his messenger darkness eternal, the primal fire of liberation, Seker-Set-Heh!

# PART III

# What is Pathworking

**by Judith Page**

You can look upon this pathworking as an initiatory experience such as the one explained in *Pilgrimage* by Paul Coelho that will open in the seeker a genuine and true dimension of what a real quest and initiation is all about.

You will find that this pathworking will aid you to unfold the quest within since you are both the quest and the path. The goal of initiatory pathworking is the direct awakening of your consciousness to a higher level. It will involve change, perhaps welcome, perhaps not, but the transmutation of stagnant and outworn energies will occur within the crucible of your soul. It will also reveal to you an awakening into a new world through the eyes of an older one. You can look upon the Neters as masters: 'When the disciple is ready, the Master appears,' so, strange encounters and inexplicable events that take place in the pathworking may alter your states of awareness and open a way of self-initiation. It can happen suddenly, awakening your very soul to your true self. You *will* become the alchemist seeking the Philosopher's Stone, seeing all in front of you with clarity and honesty but ever mindful of the Great Work.

There are several forms of pathworking known as active and passive. Active engages the mental power and tends to be directed. This is the most common magical technique taught in occult schools as it takes control of the thought processes. Using a set of intellectually understood symbols active contemplation guides the seeker along a specific thought process toward a realisation or a spiritual goal. The pathworking known as passive is where the images are allowed to rise at will once the mind has been focused on the opening symbol. Some symbols and images can get very complicated and are not always as they seem. Unless you are completely familiar with them, they may prove confusing. This type of pathworking is of more use to an advanced student of the magical arts as one is likely to go off on tangents and can get very easily lost in strange or bizarre associations that may prove tricky to extract oneself from. If this should occur, you should push away the association you recognise as taking you away from your goal. Stay calm and refocus, which should get you back on track.

All pathworking journeys have a beginning, middle, and end. Yours will always begin in front of two great pylons, a portal between them to enter leaving your world behind, and then return to your own realm. These pylons should be built with love and care. You will recognize each stone and marking on them. Think of the great pylons at the entrance of Karnak Temple as you build yours. Visualise the pale gold of the sandstone and smell the warmth of the sunlight as it falls on it.

Imagine feeling the coolness as you pass through the portal and into a landscape that will take you into the heart of ancient Khemit. You will learn how to focus on its energy as you are drawn in. This is the type of structure you will envisage each time you go on your journey. Your pylons will be your safeguard.

You will end your journey much as you began it, and return to the mundane world through the pylons, hearing the gates close behind you. It is important to hear those gates closing, so click your fingers and stamp your feet. Many problems can occur if the gates are not properly closed. It is just common sense and makes for good psychic hygiene. Doorways have been opened both mentally and on the astral level, and you need to ensure nothing comes through that is going to negatively affect either you or your environment.

Not only will you be going on a pathworking but a crossing into the soul of the temple. It will give you an insight into the god who will impart to you the secrets and mysteries that lay within the culture of this ancient land. You will learn to merge in with the environment and interact with the main players, the Neter, Anpu. He is real and potent energy, stripped bare of millennia of our projected desires, hopes, and misconceptions. Approach him with respect and you will find the way that opens before you.

As you embark on your pathworking, your guide will be Djehuty; many readers will know him as Thoth. He was not only the god of writing and knowledge but was believed in ancient times to have been a time lord.

Djehuty symbolises many things, balance, truthfulness, complete knowledge, and wisdom, being 'Lord of the Holy Words' holding the power to create and destroy. With Him you the seeker will find many doors being opened and much that is hidden brought to light. All that is asked of you is that you are honest and sincere in your efforts to seek knowledge – of yourself and the universe.

As you work with the individual Neter during your pathworking you will be mindful of ritual elements; blessings; consecrations; hymns and most important of all, their name. As Kagemni, a 6th Dynasty philosopher wrote: 'He holds fast to the Neter's name and inspires others to meditate on it.'

In addition to the common name of the god, like Anubis for Anpu, they also had a hidden name, a name of power that the priests and priestesses used in ritual. In your pathworking your magical name will be revealed to you for you to use throughout. It will be known only to you and the Neter and should not be revealed to anyone else. Certain secrets revealed, soon lose their power.

At times you may be aware of others being with you as they too travel through the ancient land of Khemit. They may appear as shadows, or shades, you may even hear them whispering within the temple precincts. If this disturbs you, then build your pylons and leave through the portal back to your realm. You can always return when you feel the time is right.
If on the other hand you are interrupted, visualise your temple pylon and step back through the portal to your physical level remembering always to seal it after you.
Like names, words also had great power, especially in the ancient language of Egypt. This should not be dismissed lightly. Scientists

today have discovered that sounds have power, and when vibrated at the right frequency they can either change or destroy matter. The Word embodies potent power.

As you explore this temple and sacred places in your pathworking, you will be aware of passing into a different field of energy. The architects of ancient Egypt were not just designing a structure to house a god they were building on a physical power zone. Each zone not only absorbed a special current of vital energy from the physical environment, but also from higher levels of cosmic consciousness. The phenomenon known as time operated in a uniquely different way within these temples.

You may be familiar with the phrase 'as above, so below.' To the ancient Egyptians, they were building heaven on earth. The temple is built over the power spot that would amass the magic working in it for hundreds of years. The power from that spot would seep into the temple walls and would be self-perpetuating, kept alive by devotion and ritual. The Egyptian temple was likened to a machine for maintaining and developing divine energy.

You may ask what happens when a temple is pulled down or moved to another place. That power would still be there. Remember that the ancient Egyptians would sometimes take an older temple apart and incorporate the stones into the walls and foundations of another one far away. This would be a way of getting stones already imbued with the power to pre-charge the new temple.

Are you prepared to surrender yourself?

# Path to Anubis

### by Judith Page & Jan Malique

Don your white robe and tie brown and black cords around your waist. This will be in respect of the Neter you will be working with. Build your pylons and make the sign of the ankh in the air above your head. On the lintel of the portal, hieroglyphs of Anpu will appear.

An-pu

Commit them to memory. This symbol is charged, look at each mark and take it within. As you utter your secret name your journey takes you to where the great Temple of Anpu can be found. It is here where you will commune with the god. This is a gateway that will take you to the heart of his realm. You will learn how to focus on his energy as you are drawn in.

You emerge into a twilight world. It is silent, remote, vast, and mysterious. The scent of evaporating heat hits your nostrils, intermingled with that of aromatic herbs. You stand for a while just drinking it in.

The air about you becomes very still, unnaturally so, which makes you slightly nervous. You wonder where your guide is. Suddenly the touch of a hand on your elbow makes you jump. Djehuty's smiling eyes twinkle down at you. You take his hand and walk towards a great temple that looms out of the darkness. In ancient times it was known as Hardai.

Djehuty looks at you shrewdly and speaks in measured tones.
'Pilgrim, this si the moment you have been waiting for even

asking for. When you, the pilgrim seek answers. When the pulses from your heart reach me, and I answer.' even asking for. When you, the pilgrim seek answers. When the pulses from your heart reach me, and I answer.'

Fear and uncertainty rise from your solar plexus making you stumble, and you tighten the grip on your guardian's hand. You hear an inner voice within saying:

'It is too soon, too soon.'

'Too soon, too soon!' mocks the wind. Even nature scorns your fears! Phosphorescent stars light up the velvety darkness. Djehuty scans the surroundings quickly and urges you onwards.

You approach the main entrance to the temple via pylon gates, sheer polished walls tower majestically towards the night sky, four flag poles are contained within niches in the walls, and their flags flutter strangely in a now windless night. To your eyes the temple appears to be suspended in the middle of a starlit lake, the flagstaff that surmounts the soaring pylons on each side of the main entrance, now stripped of their coloured banners, reflects downward to the underworld as well as upward to the overarching sky.

Your guide appears nervous.

'We must reach the place of Judgement on time, but first, it is necessary for you to commune with your Heart before we begin.'

Djehuty places a heart scarab in your hand. You look at him with surprise... understanding dawns. So it begins...

You move on to formal gardens, and even in the low light you can see flower beds, their heady perfume fills the air around you.

The area is vast, larger than you had imagined. The layout consists of a series of enclosed halls, open courts, and entrance pylons aligned along a path used for festival processions. The sacred lake is still and inky black, mirroring the stars from the sky above.

'In my ibis form, I will drink from the waters here that will serve to purify it. It is then ready for the priesthood to make their ablutions to their bodies before they enter the sanctum of Anpu.' Djehuty stands for a moment in silent contemplation, and says, 'The priesthood will make eight ritual bathings; the first being before dawn in readiness to clean, dress and feed the lord Anpu in his shrine. Come, Pilgrim, but before we continue, cover your head with this veil.'

He leads you into the great hypostyle hall. Even in the low light, you can make out the many columns all standing in shadowy rows decorated from the base to the top in green, blue, and red and wreathed with banners.

Torches flicker from the walls and display gold stars of the goddess Nut painted on a lapis lazuli blue ceiling. The sacred temple walls are covered with engravings of Anpu. Other walls depict malicious animals and reptile creatures being hacked by daggers to keep them forever still. Now they stand in a silent watch. It is easy to be quiet in such a place. The images graven on the wall seem impregnated with the scent of sandalwood and frankincense. The forms of worship all lead to the same goal, which is both spiritual as it is set in motion and practical in the final awaited results of supplication and offerings. This grand building aims to be purely functional, a divine machine for the adoration of a being, the god Anpu.

A wistful reed pipe begins to call. Instinct tells you to follow the sound. Someone else is present in this strange, hushed hour. But your attention is drawn elsewhere.

Within the gloom of this house of power is the sanctuary that holds the god.

A priest, dressed in ritual clothing is present. Through your veil you see him as he lights a torch. This is associated with the eye of Horus. The priest adds more incense to a brazier to purify the air. He does not speak, only nods his head in recognition and leads you past the great pylons that represent the horizon, and proceeds to the inner sanctuary.

During this passage the priest awakens the temple, bringing it and its deities to life in a ritual of similar form to the ritual of the opening of the mouth from the funerary literature.

Before the doors of the sanctum, the priest chants a prayer as he removes the curtain covering this entrance, then pulls back the bolt from the door to the holy of holies, and utters,

'May the pulling of this bolt represent the removing of the finger of Set from the eye of Horus. May the opening of these doors of the sanctuary be as 'heaven', and may we see the face of the god.' More fumigations are wafted in the direction of the sanctuary.

'I present thee with offerings to restore the eye of Horus.'

All the while your heartbeat is thudding in your ears. Whispering phantoms from the shadows want answers from you.

'Why do you enter this sanctum?' they chime in unison.

You make to reply but you are distracted by a figure emerging from the shadows.

'Who goes there?' It is the voice of the High Priest.

'I am a seeker,' you reply, your voice quavering.

'You are a dweller of the outer darkness where ignorance lives. Are you worthy?'

*Are* you worthy Pilgrim? Think before you reply.

'I am worthy.'

'The Path to initiation is treacherous and filled with trials and temptation. Are you willing to take it?'

'I am.'

'What do you seek?'

'I seek initiation.'

The High Priest falls silent.

You wait. Have you said something wrong? *You seek more,* prompting a voice from within you.

'I seek the mystery of past ages,' you state clearly.

You hear the High Priest sigh, followed by other low voices. He is joined by a figure in dark robes whose bowed head causes the low light to obscure his features. As the High Priest lifts the veil from your face the other figure proffers a cup to your lips. You hesitate before drinking. *What if it's poison?* You think.

'Drink the scented wine, child,' urges the High Priest. 'It will soothe the hurts and wounds which may arise from the depths of your heart.'

You do as he commands.

You drink from the cup and feel the sweet liquid slide down your throat.

The High Priest's voice drones on.

You are suddenly nervous as you realise that Djehuty has disappeared.

The High Priest reads your thoughts and says:

'I will be your guide from now hence, protecting your inner levels. I will teach you ancient by-laws of the sacred mystery schools.'

You tighten the grip around the heart scarab that nestles

safely in your left hand, then, you drift off into a deep sleep.

You find yourself walking along a long corridor, dimly lit by torches, the smell of sandalwood and frankincense incense weaving between the pillars, becoming ever stronger as you reach a doorway at the end of this never-ending corridor. Protective hieroglyphs are deeply etched all around the lintel, as you commit them to memory the scarab in your hand starts to pulse. This does not disturb you, rather it serves only to reassure. You go through the doorway to be met by a priest, robed in gold and black. His features are finely sculpted, with a full mouth and deep, dark eyes. He watches you intently, then, a smile breaks the solemnity of his gaze.

'You are exactly how I imagined you to be.'

You wonder who he is and before you can ask, he replies,

'I am the guardian of that most sacred temple you call your heart. You have served the god within well, have no worries on that account.

Before you entered this world, I have guarded this holy place, nurtured it, loved it, and birthed it.'

His words make you catch your breath and tears well up in your eyes. He continues:

'To be true to your heart is more precious to you than any riches this world or the next could offer.'

The priest looks at you and nods his head. Yes, perhaps now is the time to express that, which has remained hidden within this most precious temple. You want to say so much, that you hear yourself utter:

'I present myself, stripped bare of any artifice, embellishments, and subterfuges. It has been a life less than perfect, filled with pain, disappointment, and regret. My pride has caused me to fall many times and my anger extinguished many a hope. Compassion and mercy have flown to the winds on many occasions and wisdom is buried beneath the sands. I have not heeded the words of those who are wiser than myself and like a headstrong child have stumbled on obstacles of my making. Yet, hope drives me on, for:

Without a memory of my beloved Khemit,
    I should be nothing.
    Without the love of my most beloved Neters,

> I should be nothing.
> Without humanity,
> I should be nothing.

My heart has felt much which has been dark, but the glorious light of Ra has shone within its recesses, illuminating its beauty, joy, and grace. This much I have offered others. Will you accept me as I am?'

The heart scarab begins to pulsate rhythmically, and with each pulse, you feel a ripple of energy flow outwards from your own heart. The very heart of the known and unknown is contained within yourself, and it is a doorway you feel compelled to go through. Dare you take that leap of faith? You focus the energy on your heart centre using it as a key. Then, you feel a surging move through your body.

After what seems like æons, a hand on your shoulder gently brings the present into focus. It is time to enter the chamber of judgement – the Weighing of the Heart begins. Figures line the walls on either side, only their outlines are visible, and the rest is lost in shadow. Not so! A group of figures wait at the other end of the chamber, majesty and power emanate from them, bathed in golden light they are set apart from all which is of the mundane world. They watch silently and without expression. You are beckoned to come forward, only to find the chamber has dissolved and stars surround you on all sides.

Djehuty moves into view, scroll and stylus ready in hand. Ma'at stands to one side and as you look beyond them, Anpu sits majestically upon a golden throne. Your heart leaps within your breast at the dog-god's magnificence.

You stand transfixed, looking at him. You feel the eyes of the god upon you, weighing up your future. You may have been to the Temple of Karnak and you may have been moved by its grandeur, but this being that stands before you emits energy that comes in waves passing over you, yet has no physical form.

A voice from within speaks, 'It is our core spiritual nature, our inner self. ... Inner Beings often show themselves in a form that they know will resonate and be trusted by their human incarnations – that is us.'

Anpu was ancient when Osiris swept into the land of Khemit, 'Lord of the Hallowed Land' and 'Foremost of the Westerners'.

Impassive eyes scrutinise with thoroughness, there is nowhere to hide. He is resplendent in obsidian blackness, strongly sculpted jackal head, broad shoulders sweeping down to muscular hips draped with a gold kilt, and as always, the Uwas sceptre in his right hand. He is absolute power and authority, not to be trifled with.

Ammit, the Devourer lurks oppressively in the gloom, too awful to face, yet inescapable. There is no movement for what seems like an eternity then you are asked to place the heart scarab on the scale. Ma'at takes the feather out of her headdress and places it on the other side.

Djehuty's measured tones ring out, 'The time has come to account for your life, be open, be truthful. Seek neither to prevaricate nor fabricate. We know all and we see all. Begin.'

The scroll of your life unravels, bit by bit, the hieroglyphs burn on the surface of the papyrus, glowing with intensity.

They are on fire!

An entire lifetime is encapsulated in this one moment, the words flow onwards manifesting in almost forgotten scenes, some uplifting, and others unbearable in their clarity. Such was earthly life, a myriad of transformative experiences.

Out of the corner of your eye, you glimpse Djehuty's stylus continuing to fly across the papyrus, ceaselessly recording every utterance. Will you be declared 'true of voice'?

His stylus stops.

All eyes focus on the gigantic scales that are traced out by stars in the expanse of the heavens.

The delicate balancing of the scales must not be hurried. The vibration of your heartbeats echoes loudly, deep and sonorous, hypnotic in their rhythm.

A pronouncement is made and whether it is acceptable or not, is for you, and only you, to judge. It will have a great bearing on the life which is to come. This has *not* been a judgement but initiation, most profound.

Mighty Anpu steps down from his throne and approaches you. The earth shakes with each step he takes. Banish all preconceptions you have of this ancient Neter; he is son to no one, no mere psycho pomp but the Great Initiator, Lord of the Underworld. He gestures for your heart to be returned. A tightly bound papyrus is also handed to you – the contents of which are known only to you. He speaks and you listen:

'Remember that life is a series of what you may call challenges, but these are not in continuous motion. There must be periods of quiet reflection. Time to think, breathe and feel and to understand how far you have travelled on this, *your* journey. Life begins with reason, it has a purpose, but what is the greatest shame is that you forget these reasons almost as soon as you are born.' He pauses, then continues,

'Life on earth is so full of the complex issues of survival, we do not remember that there is a purpose behind the chaos I call life. However, as you are aware, from chaos comes order. There are opportunities for you to grow or stay in what I call a state of neediness. Life is full of many materialistic views and therefore occupies your mind more than the spiritual pathways that you should be taking. When the time is right, change will occur. Receive my blessings and prosper well.'

Djehuty appears by your side as the stars fade and the solid walls of the chamber take shape once more.

It is time to take leave of this sacred space and return to your own time and place. To linger too long in the realm of the dead is to bring many calamities upon yourself.

What have you learnt? Have you understood what Anpu has said to you? Will it change your perception of what existence and consciousness actually are?

Soon the temple doors loom into view, and you are ushered into the already bright dawn. The morning air is ripe with dew and the glorious face of Ra is steadily rising in the skies. You bid your guide farewell until the next encounter.

Utter your secret name to the gods, go through the portal into your world and seal the door behind you.

# Meaning of Invoking

### by Judith Page

*'In the beginning was the Word,*
*the Word was with God,*
*and the Word was God.'*

Invocations are both spiritual and practical. There are very few times in ritual where you do not invoke Gods. But, before you can invoke a God, you must first know just what it is that you are invoking. These invocations and meditations are not empty verbalisms; they greatly enhance and enrich our lives as we enter into their realm.

Working with the energies of a Neter can be powerful and enlightening. There are many ways you can work with these ancient gods, and many reasons for doing so. For example, you may be faced with an upcoming event in your life that you could use some support and encouragement and connecting with a powerful god can help bring these elements to aid your situation.

Sometimes there are situations where you have lost or given away your power to someone or something. Invoking a Neter can help connect you with inner forces thereby pushing away boundaries and restoring assertiveness.

By the act of invoking, you are communicating with the god using words, thoughts, and feelings and you are open to receiving any messages. Whatever connection you make, you may find that the very association is healing and empowering.

Using invocations, we are also attempting to create a stargate to pass through, whereby you can communicate and aspire not only to become one with the gods again but enter into other dimensions.

We are also attempting to reveal through invocation how an ancient Egyptian would interact with a god. Using the ancient Egyptian language you will summon or call up the god through the use of speech. Why in Egyptian, you ask?

The Egyptians claimed the Gods or Neteru gave their language to them directly from the Spiritual World. Like all languages, ancient Egyptian has similarities and common roots shared with some other ancient languages. The Copts still use the ancient Egyptian language to pray. However, Egyptians claimed that the very sounds that make up their language are themselves Powers, and that claim should not be dismissed lightly.

We already know that sound has the power to break glass and pulverize rock. Sound is used to break up kidney stones within the body, without the need for surgery, and sound can make us feel happy or sad, well or extremely ill. The power of sound is undeniable. We know that the very matter of the universe resonates with vibration. Why then, wouldn't it be possible that the universe we know is created by sound, which in its most basic definition is just a vibration?

It is the hope that future generations of scientists may yet discover that sounds are powers in their own right. According to Jerry Clifford Welch, *Hebet En Ba: The Book of Rites*, 'Egyptian "divinity" may very well still "speak" the Egyptian tongue and will be listening to our utterances! It is through these utterances we will connect with the Gods'.

As you work with the individual god or Neter during your invocations, you will be mindful of ritual elements, blessings, consecrations, hymns and most important of all, the Neter's name.

**The word Neter and its meaning**
When the term Gods is used regarding the ancient Egyptians, it is a misrepresentation of their term Neteru.

The Egyptians gave the name Neter to the great and supreme power, this 'One God', that which made the earth, the heavens, the sea, the sky, men and women, animals, birds, and creeping things, all that is and all that shall be.

They felt that to know this 'One God' was to know the many faces and qualities of this entity, and the more they learned of these faces, the closer they got to the divine origin. This One God was self-produced, self-existent, invisible, eternal, omniscient, almighty, and immortal. Although this One God was never represented, the functions and attributes of his domain were represented in the many forms of the Neteru. The difference between the conceptions of Neter, the one supreme God, and the Neteru is best shown by an appeal to Egyptian texts.

*'In the pyramid of Unas it is said to the deceased, un-k ar kes Neter. Thou existest at the side of God.'*

It should also be pointed out that the Egyptian culture lasted over 3000 years. This is a fact that many forget when they begin learning about the Neters. They never seem to realise that things change over three millennia.

Over time, stories and Gods were essential to explain events and situations that could not otherwise be explained, or to give divine right to someone or something. New Gods were encountered as the Egyptians traded with other cultures, and by combining two or more Neters together they found a better match for their needs.

This is not unusual. One only has to look at the changes Christianity has gone through in two-thirds of that time. It is a normal part of history that people also change, and so do their spiritual needs. The Egyptians simply adapted their Neters to best suit the needs of the people as they saw fit. Understanding this will help you to retain your focus on the Neter, and not on the name used.

**Invocational Rites**
In ancient Egypt, the priests of the temples performed daily Invocational Rites to the statues of the Neters. These rituals were elaborate and were held in the morning, noon and at night.
In the morning, the ritual was designed to awaken the Neter, feed it, bathe it and clothe it, while the evening ritual was designed to

put the Neter to bed. Clothes, food, drink, and incense were all essential parts of the Invocational Rite, and each rite was several hours accompanied by equally long litanies.

In these modern times we do not have the luxury to enter into such exhaustive daily rituals. In doing so, we would never leave the temple or shrine! Hence, we have developed Invocational Rites, that take the essence of the rituals of the temple, so that we can honour the Gods in a similar way as the Ancient Egyptians, while still maintaining our daily routines *and* experience and developing a relationship with the Neter.

Practically all Invocational Rites use a few basic principles that are, in fact, truths in themselves, principles that work upon their intended subjects, even though you may not yourself be able to hear or see the sense of it all! Many traditions of magic today still use such rites, for example, Kabbalah, which means 'receiving'. Most having been arrived at independently by cultures from different continents and ages in history, these principles should be accepted as simply working methodologies, rather than anything to believe or believe in.

The principles of all Invocation occur within a sacred space that can be metaphysically drawn or created by the practitioner for the occasion and erased or banished to release the powers to go on with their performing of the work, the rite requested of them.

The ancient Egyptians were known to have employed the use of sacred space within their rites where the Gods were invoked or called upon and asked to manifest themselves. This was done via ritual, which involved the invocation of the First Time (Zep Tepi) that, according to Jung, was seen as an existence outside of this reality.
In later times the four deities or Neteru, that represented the equivalent of the four quarters: Tuameutev (East), Amset (South), Qebsenuv (West), and Hapi (North), were invoked to guard a sacred space.

Aleister Crowley states that: To 'invoke' is to 'call in' just as to 'evoke' is to 'call forth'. This is the essential difference between the two branches of magic. In invocation, the macrocosm floods the consciousness. In evocation, the magician, having become the macrocosm, creates a microcosm.

As already discussed, the universe was the macrocosm and the body was the microcosm. Hence the top of the head corresponded to the top of the universe, the North Star. Ascension macro cosmically through the heavens (often numbered as seven) to the highest heaven corresponded to ascension microcosmically of the fire-snake (kundalini), the primal source, or power that usually lays dormant in the non-initiate.

According to Iamblicus, Theurgia or On the Mysteries of Egypt:
*'It is through evoking higher spiritual powers by means of rites of Supernatural Magic that humans come to a true realization of what they are in essence: eternal spiritual entities.'*

There are two primary methods of invocation, the first being the traditional western method which is devotional, and the second being the Egyptian method whereby the personality of the God-form is awakened from the beginning by the invoker.

Learn to recognize the connection, don't create it, the connection is always there, you are just unaware of it most of the time. Day-to-day issues and concerns distract you from feeling the connection.

Don't worry if nothing seems to happen, it takes time and practice, but everyone has the ability.

Once you get to the point where you *do* recognize the connection to Deity, make your mind perfectly still and open to the Divine, call out to the God or Goddess you wish to invoke and feel a shift in the connection when they answer.

As a colleague of mine, Ken Biles rightly said: 'When you invoke a God or Goddess, you are invoking part of yourself. You are communicating with that part of you that is Divine'.
Invocation – meaning

*Pronunciation:* (in"vu-kā'shun)
1. the act of invoking or calling upon a deity, spirit, etc., for aid, protection, inspiration, or the like; request.
2. any petitioning or request for help or aid.
3. a form of prayer invoking God's presence, especially one said at the beginning of a religious service or public ceremony.
4. an entreaty for aid and guidance from a muse, deity, etc., at the beginning of an epic or epic-like poem.
5. the act of calling upon a spirit by incantation.
6. the magic formula used to conjure up a spirit; incantation.
7. the act of calling upon or referring to something, as a concept or document, for support and justification in a particular circumstance.
8. the enforcing or use of a legal or moral precept or right.

**Practical Matters**
Preparation:
There are several versions of the Invocation Rite, but all are similar in many ways, which include:
- ~ The ritual washing
- ~ The wearing of white clothes
- ~ The offering of incense
- ~ The offering of water, food, and drink

There is, however, a practical side of invocation. Consider the business of your own space and time. Most of us do not have much of either. Few of us have spare rooms where we can isolate ourselves for meditation or invocation. Above all, many of us have to be discreet in our activities.

What might you need? We suggest you wear a plain white robe made from natural material such as cotton or linen for example. White is the colour of purity in Ancient Egypt. Wearing white shows that you are ritually pure. You can either choose to buy it or make it yourself. But, it must be your robe – no one else must be allowed to wear it. You should wear that robe for invocation/ritual, nothing else. Putting on that robe symbolizes that you are putting aside the mundane world and stepping into the world of the spirit. As you will be working with numerous different Neters, we suggest you wear a coloured sash or cord corresponding to a particular Neter.

## Cleansing

Before doing any magical work we always recommend to people to take a shower, or preferably a long, hot soaking bath. One tradition is to bless salt and mix it into the water, thus exorcising the water of any energies other than cleansing ones.

You may want to make up a small sachet of mixed crushed herbs and drop them into the bath so that you can breathe in their odours while you bathe.

Play soothing music, burn appropriate incense, light candles, or add any other elements you like that will reinforce two primary ideas: 1) getting rid of all previous thoughts and obsessions, and 2) beginning to focus on the energies to be worked with in the upcoming rite.

When you get out of the shower/bath put on your white robe and without letting your mind drift too far into other topics, go straight to the place where you will be doing your invocations.

The sanctuary of the Neter was usually approached through a hall, entered via an open-air courtyard. This marked the transition from the human realm to that of the divine.

In terms of our modern lifestyle and houses, we can still emerge cleansed from the primal waters (bath or shower) and walk through the house (courtyard and hall) to enter the divine sanctuary to perform our rites (temple room).

## Altar

Clear a surface that functions as your altar. For this, you will need a pair of candlesticks, a supply of candles, and something that serves as an altar cloth. You might want an incense burner. An ancient Egyptian priest would have used an incense 'spoon'. The deep bowl would have held charcoal and incense. The priest would have picked up the spoon and raised it to the nose of a statue. He would have announced that prayers and incense had reached the God.

As charcoal gets very hot and stays that way for a long time, a metal bowl containing charcoal can char a table, and a glass bowl will crack with the heat. We, therefore, suggest one made of earthenware. To keep the base of the bowl cool, put a layer of sand about one inch thick in the bottom of the receptacle, then place the prepared charcoal on the sand. For further protection of surfaces, make sure the incense burner is placed on an insulated or fireproof mat or trivet.

Remember that very little incense goes a long way. Think of a small salt spoon. One salt spoon full of incense may be sufficient for your invocation, especially in a small room. Working in a fog of incense smoke is not recommended, as it will penetrate a house or flat. Some people cannot tolerate this type of smoke so you may want to consider using an oil vaporizer instead. These can be purchased from most shops. You will need a packet of tea lights, which can be purchased from a supermarket.

The candle goes under the bowl that contains water followed by a few drops of scented oil. This will fragrance a room without smoke to worry other people. It is also less of a health and fire risk.

For those who cannot burn incense, use essential oil. The pleasing smell is what is needed. In terms of candles, if you cannot burn them, find an appropriate substitute, such as a low-light candle lamp or dimmed lights.

Obtain a statuette or picture of the Neter with whom you are seeking contact. Be practical and realistic in your expectations, and if your budget is constrained, a picture of the Neter can serve as a focus for your worship just as well. It is the sincerity of your feelings not the depth of your wallet that is important.

## Offerings
In Ancient Egyptian culture, nothing was wasted. Once the food had been offered up to the Neter, the spirit of the deity entered this

offering. The physical portion of the food was consumed by the priests of the temple, or in the case of festivals, given to the people gathered outside the temple. If you include food on your altar, ensure that this offering *is* consumed afterwards. If not by you, then by another, be it animal or person.

**Rhythmic Breathing Practice**
Rhythmic breathing improves the chances of success in spiritual development. Atoms, the earth, the solar system, and everything in the universe has their own vibration or rhythm. The body has rhythms too. By breathing rhythmically, you are helping your body work as nature intended, and in doing so you absorb a great deal more of its life-force energy.

According to the ancient Egyptians, practicing rhythmic breathing attuned them to the rhythm of the universe, rhythmic breathing helped them establish a sense of oneness with the Gods.

The benefits of rhythmic breathing are:
>    Increased oxygen supply (even more than deep breathing)
>    Re-establishes the body's own natural rhythm

Rhythmic breathing, as well as correct concentration and meditation, can bring about a great change in both your physical and mental state and serve as a step toward spiritual unfolding.

It was understood by the Egyptians that deep rhythmic breathing exercises followed the rhythm of the body allowing the body to absorb a lot more oxygen than just normal deep breathing.

The practice of deep rhythmic breathing exercises will allow our body to re-establish its own natural rhythm and attune us more to the cosmic rhythm. This will protect us from any negative external influences.

Rhythmic breathing is achieved in the same way as deep breathing, but it is timed to the rhythm of your heartbeat.

Inhalation and exhalation should be done to the same number of beats, as this establishes an even rhythm. It is interesting to note that the Ancient Egyptians believed that the heart provided channels (metu) that linked all parts of the body together. These channels delivered not only blood but air.

**Technique**
Sit comfortably on a chair keeping the spine straight, with your hands on your knees, and start by taking a few deep breaths – and stop. Put the fingers of your right hand on your left wrist to find the pulse.

Carefully listen to the pulse beat, and after a short while start counting 1-2-3-4 several times to the rhythm of the beats.

Continue mentally counting 1-2-3-4, 1-2-3-4 until you fall into this rhythm and can follow it without holding your pulse. Put your hands on your knees and take a deep breath while counting 1-2-3-4; hold the breath while counting 1-2; exhale while again counting 1-2-3-4.

Inhale slowly and deeply for eight seconds. Push your stomach forwards to a count of four seconds, push your ribs sideways for a count of two seconds, and finally lift your chest and collarbone upwards to a count of two seconds. This makes a total of eight seconds.

Don't breathe out immediately, instead, hold the breath for four seconds, this is called retention.

Exhale slowly for eight seconds. For the first six seconds just allow the collarbone, chest and ribs to relax, so that the breath goes out automatically.

For the last two seconds, push the stomach in gently to expel air from the lungs. Keep the stomach in this position for four seconds before you take the next breath.

Do the above exercise three times the first week, and add one more round each week, until you achieve seven breaths.
**Rhythmic Breathing with Visualisation**

The rhythmic breathing exercise is made much more potent if you use visualisation while doing the breathing, this also aids invocations.

Visualisation works on the belief that whatever you concentrate on, an extra supply of oxygen will be directed to that area. The secret of successful invocation is combining the exercise with visualising the specific area the exercise affects.

The technique is simple. When you breathe in, visualize the life force accumulating in the solar plexus area, just above the navel, behind the stomach. The solar plexus is where the body stores its energy. When you retain the breath and breathe out, visualize the life force going to the brain. Just concentrate on the brain area.

This visualization technique achieves two things. Firstly it produces a reserve of energy in the solar plexus, thereby increasing your general energy level. Second, since some of the stored energy is directed to the brain, brain function and vitality are increased.

**Temple life**
Many people think that life in Egyptian temples was placid and tranquil but this is a vision seen through rose-tinted spectacles. The priests ran orphanages and schools. They ran the medical service via herb gardens. They ran festivals. They ran the death and burial services. White robes had to be laundered. Young priests had to be rehearsed, even if they were pulled from their sleeping mats at three in the morning. Older priests would need feeding after long vigils. Those who worked with the Neters were kept very busy indeed.

Don't be afraid of rehearsing. Invocation does not come easily to many people. The greatest magicians and high priests have all had to start at the beginning. All had to practice before they became legendary figures. They all trained and sweated to achieve magnificent results.

Be realistic about your goals, pace yourself, and learn to 'see' from different viewpoints, for truth can be multi-layered. Remember not to lose your sense of humour amidst the hurly-burly of magical activity. The Gods may see fit to trip you up to deflate your ego now and again!

How often should an invocation be done? No two invocations are alike in their approach to this practice, so some method of monitoring is suggested. Keeping a diary will also be a valuable record of the development of your magical personality, as over time you are able to chart your progress, amend working methods and discard those that do not work. For beginners, one working per week is sufficient. Invocation is not designed to take over your life, and as with everything else, should be done in moderation. The invocations will impact upon your inner and outer worlds, profoundly in the case of certain deities, so cultivate patience. A seedling tended with care, love, and patience soon develops into a strong and healthy plant, just like the developing divine consciousness.

We have taken a brief look at the practical side of invocation. Let us consider the more spiritual side of working as we invoke Anpu.

# Invoking Anubis

by Judith Page

**What you will need:**
Oil of frankincense, incense, charcoal, goblet of wine/beer, fruit juice or water, two black candles, a statue or picture of the Neter, and a small scarab of any material.

**Preparation:**
Don your white robe and tie a brown and black cord around your waist. This will be in respect of Anpu the Neter you will be invoking. Anoint wrists, temples, and throat with oil of frankincense. Light candles. Prepare charcoal and add incense as required. Fill the goblet with liquid and raise it in salutation to Anpu, and place it back on your altar.

Meditate for a while on the hieroglyph of his name:

An-pu

Sit comfortably in an upright chair and commence rhythmic breathing for 4 to 6 rounds.

Say temple prayer to deity:
> 'Sesenet neftu nedjem
> Per em rek
> Peteri nefruk em menet
> Ta-i nehet sedj emi
> Kheruk nedjem en mehit
> Renpu ha-i em ankh
> en mertuk.

'I breathe the sweet breath
Which comes forth from thy mouth.
I behold thy beauty every day
It is my desire
That I may be rejuvenated
With life, through love of thee.

Di-ek eni awik kher ka-ek
Shesepi su ankhi yemef
I ashek reni er heh
Ben hehif em rek.'

Give me thy hands, holding thy spirit,
That I may receive it and may live by it.
Call thou upon my name unto eternity,
And it shall never fail.'

Invocation:

'Hail to thee Anpu
True and mighty Lord of the Underworld.
I have journeyed far on a quest and now find myself at the gates of his sacred temple.
Prepared am I to face the tests you have prepared and petition for entry into the Hall of Judgement.'

*All is quiet as you await a sign that your petition has been heard. The creak of mighty gates opening breaks the silence and you find yourself standing in a twilight world. It is remote, vast and mysterious.*
*Add a little incense to the charcoal; the scent hits your nostrils, intermingled with that of aromatic herbs. Stand for a while just drinking it in. Take a small sip of liquid from your goblet. Reflect, and commune with your heart before the weighing begins. It is a chance to honestly face your true self, Your Heart, and declare all that you have been and choose to be. Say:*

'I drink from the cup,
May it serve to stimulate lost memories,
May it soothe the hurts and wounds that may arise from the

depths of my heart.
May the aromas of sandalwood and frankincense surround me.
May I be permitted to pass through the double pillars, one black and one white,
May the protective hieroglyphs impact my senses as I commit them to memory.
I call upon the guardian of that most sacred temple you call, My Heart.
Thou who hast guarded this holy place since the time I entered this world.
Thou who hast nurtured and loved it, loved it and birthed it.
Bless me I pray thee, for I have served the God within, well.
I present myself before you, stripped bare of any artifice embellishments and subterfuges.
It has been a life less than perfect, filled with pain, disappointment and regret.
My pride has caused me to fall many times and my anger extinguished many a hope.
Compassion and mercy have flown to the winds on many occasions and wisdom is buried beneath the sands.
I have not heeded the words of those who are wiser than myself and like a headstrong child have stumbled on obstacles of my making.
Yet, hope drives me on, for:

Without memory of my beloved Khemit,
I should be nothing.
Without love of my most beloved Neters,
I should be nothing.
Without humanity,
I should be nothing.

My heart has felt much, which has been dark
But the glorious light of Ra has shone within its recesses, illuminating its beauty, joy and grace.
This much I have offered others.
Will you accept me as I am?

The very heart of the known and unknown is contained within

myself,
It is but a doorway I will journey through.'

*Pause here; reflect upon all that has brought you to this moment. For what is to come will be a revelation if not life-changing. Remember that you have entered the realm of the dead, a place fraught with dangers if not navigated properly, stay focused and calm.*

Nuk per ami-ab
Pre-ab ami- kshat,
Anksh-a em T'ett'a-a.

I, coming forth am pure of heart
Within the pure of body,
I live through my words.

Sem – a em sentet en kshertu,
Sekeru – na
Ar eq – kua er seta
Au eh-he hah Tet hru ent Anpu
Kshesev neseni, t'a pa ma-ehti!

I have made my way by way of the Tree of Life,
And I have brought myself to silence.
Now I have entered into The Sacred Mysteries
And standing behind the Throne on the day of Anpu
Driving back disaster sail forth the right and truth!

*The time approaches for the Judgement to begin. Make your way into the great chamber.*

As the Weighing of my Heart begins,
May the Neters fill the chamber I stand within.
May these invisible watchers observe the judgement.
I pray that their majesty and power give me strength.
May I be justly bathed in the golden light that emanates from them.
I feel their silent gaze upon my fragile being.

'I call upon Djehuty to mark well my life's deeds.
I call upon Ma'at.
I call upon the Great Anpu who sits upon a golden throne,
Ah, his dog-face is magnificent!
Hail Lord of the Hallowed Land!
Foremost of the Westerners
You are resplendent in obsidian blackness,
Strongly sculptured is your jackal head,
Your broad shoulders sweep down to muscular hips draped with a golden kilt.

Hail to you, great God, Lord of Justice!'

*Pause, and say:*

'May I know the names of the forty-two Gods of those who are with you in this Hall of Justice, who live on those who cherish evil and who gulp down their blood on that day of the reckoning of characters in the presence of the Great One.
Behold the double son of the Songstresses; Lord of Truth is your name.
Behold I have come to you,
I come in truth before you,
I have repelled falsehood for you.

Hark! Ammit the devourer lurks in the gloom!
Thou art awful, and inescapable.
I tremble in fear!'

*Pick up the scarab from your altar and hold it. Imagine it pulsating rhythmically, and with each pulse, you feel an energy flow outward from your own heart. Focus the energy in your heart centre using it as a key. Place the scarab back on the altar and as you do so, imagine placing it on one side of the scales, declaring:*

'I bow my head as Ma'at takes the feather from her headdress,
I watch her as she places it on the other side of the scales
Accept me as I stand here in the eternal silence awaiting my fate.'

*Djehuty says:*

'The time has come to account for your life, be open, be truthful.
Seek neither to prevaricate nor fabricate.
We know all and we see all. Begin.'

*Holding your hands out in supplication say:*

'I pray to the Neters that I may I see the scroll of my life,
Hark! I watch as my life unravels,
Bit by bit the hieroglyphs glow with intensity!

They are now on fire!
May my lifetime be encapsulated in this one moment.
May the words flow onwards manifesting in almost forgotten scenes,
May I see them clearly, some uplifting, and others unbearable in their clarity,
May I experience a myriad of transformative experiences.
I watch, as stars in the expanse of the heavens trace out the gigantic scales within my being.'

*Be quiet and stand in reflection. Take a deep breath and utter the words loudly and clearly:*

### 'MAY I BE DECLARED 'TRUE OF VOICE'

*Now begins the delicate balancing of the scales. You feel the passage of each second with trepidation. Your heartbeats echo loudly, almost hypnotic in their rhythm. Will your heart speak in your favour or will it condemn you?*

*Djehuty gives a signal and a pronouncement is finally made.*

*Mighty Anpu steps down from his throne and approaches you. The earth shakes with each step the Great Initiator makes. Piercing eyes look into yours, you have no secrets from Him, he knows all. An eternity passes, or so it seems. He gestures for your heart and a papyrus to be handed to you.*

*Anpu speaks:*
'Guard these well.
May the pronouncement be made,
Whether it be acceptable or unacceptable
It is for I, and I alone to appraise.
Let this not be a final judgement,
But the initiation of the most profound kind.'

*Say:*
'Great Initiator, Lord of the Underworld.
I pray thee, return my heart to me.'

*Anpu speaks:*
'Uhen-k nek
Urtu ab,
Pesh-k nek,
Tek-k-tu her kes-k
He-ek am-v

Arise for thyself,
O still heart,
Shine for thyself,
Stand alongside your image,
And rejoice in it.

Remember that life is a series of what you may call challenges, but these are not in continuous motion. There must be periods of quiet reflection. Time to think, breathe, feel, and understand how far you have travelled on this, *your* journey. Life begins with reason, it has a purpose, but what is the greatest shame is that you forget these reasons almost as soon as you are born. For life on earth, which is so full of the complex issues of survival, we do not remember that there is indeed purpose behind the chaos I call life. However, as you are aware, from chaos comes order. There is a purpose and there are opportunities for you to grow or stay in what I call a state of neediness. Life is full of many materialistic views and therefore occupies your mind more than the spiritual pathways that you should be taking. When the time is right, change will occur. Take my blessings and prosper well.'

*It is at this stage, that you might want to take some personal time with Anpu for meditation, quiet introspection, conversation, or whatever you need to help build and foster your relationship with this deity. The important part of this stage is to open your heart to him and enjoy his presence.*
*Bow your head and say:*

'I (utter your secret name) thank the company of Neters for aiding the weighing of my heart,
For thou hast awakened the very being from within.
May I always reflect on the judgement of 'self' and remain pure of heart.
May I realize that this purity emanates from within.'

*Stand silently, and think about what you have uttered and what has been said to you. Think of what you have been privileged to see. Close the shrine, if you have an enclosed shrine:*
*Blow out the candles*
*Remove the foodstuff; you may leave the water*
*Back away from your shrine/altar and bow.*
*Close your eyes and when you open them say these words:*

'I shall always remember that all Deities are true and valid emanations of the Supreme One and will not allow myself to become so obsessed with one aspect that I denigrate others, for this is not the true love of Deity.'


Note: Reconstructed Egyptian text from The Egyptian Book of the Dead by E. A. Wallis Budge

Paulina in the Temple of Isis (illust.70)

## Epilogue

The standard history of religion is the reformation of existing faiths. When Luther nailed his thesis to the door – he wasn't trying to get rid of Catholicism, he simply wanted to remake it. The Buddha wasn't against Hinduism, he simply wanted to simplify it. Esotericism is not about replacing a faith, or a new everything for everybody. Esotericism is about a new window for someone that is looking for or needing a new window. It is a personal affair. Some humans need enchantment, and Anubis is the shifty entity. Half of him is your desire for transcendence, not a desire for wealth or sex or social position, but a desire for otherness. He is that part of you that craves science fiction movies, the art of Dali and Spare, or even those strange things you smoked at that party. Being human, part of you longs for Otherness, but being human you want to remember your way back.

Anubis's image is found in every tomb, and every afterlife manual, and yet almost no myth mentions him. We know the stories of dozens of gods, and yet this god always remained mysterious. We know that the Egyptians were strongly visual in their understanding of their gods. They painted them. They carved them. But only Anubis has a mask. There isn't a Ra mask, an Isis mask, or a Set mask. But there are Anubis masks. It was understood that for the soul parts to reassemble after death, a certain type of ritual specialist was needed. Someone who could step *inside* of the god and appear to be the god to others.

Alone out of literally hundreds of gods Anubis is there as a Key to a certain door. Anubis lets you go where you need to go, even if you can't articulate that need. But as I pointed out above, *half* of him is created/nourished/manifested by your desire. The other half comes from outside of you. The other half is the Otherness that wants to come to you.

Have you ever been visiting a friend and their gigantic dog runs up to you and nearly knocks you down? That is your Anubis moment – as you stumble back and have your breath and thought knocked out of you. As you smell the dog breathe and the saliva drips on you, you aren't the thinking human you were seconds before. You are overcome with the Other. Anubis is not a polite god that will wait quietly in the ritual chamber. He is the demonic force imagined in Frank Long's "The Hounds of Tindalos." But at the same time, he is Falkor from *The Never Ending Story*.

This strange half and half nature of "First of the Westerners," "Lord of the Sacred Land," "He Who is Upon His Sacred Mountain," "Ruler of the Nine Bows," "The Dog who Swallows Millions," "Master of Secrets," "He Who is in the Place of Embalming," and "Foremost of the Divine Booth." Makes problematic in the ritual chamber. If you work your magic with the psychology model of "It's all in my head," I don't recommend working with Anubis. You will find he is only half in your head. Stick with something safer like Cthulhu. If on the other hand, you work with the spirit model meaning you think all those things you can name exist in reality and you are bargaining with them, Anubis doesn't work well either, half of his nature has been building up in you through comics and film and books. Anubis has been invoking you longer than you've been invoking him.

Anubis is not an abstract idea like the Greek gods, and it is notable that Plato makes Socrates swear "by the Egyptian dog" when he is wanting to make a serious point. Your approach to the Greek gods is most likely some jolly moment of childhood with an Edith Hamilton paperback in your hand and the smell of the used bookstore in your nostrils. Not so for Anubis. You came close to him visiting your grandmother at a rest home, smelling the emergency room at a hospital, or feeling the cold of a funeral home. This god cuts up your carcass in this world and not only leads you to the next but weighs your heart there. This is not a god that respects limits like your skin or your secret sins. So, this isn't a "starter" God for the young witch, a jolly idea-complex for the would-be magician, nor another god for Crowley's god-of-the-month club.

Anubis is the god that shatters barriers, and that is a good thing if you passed beyond the ego-inflating stage of magical training. If you have stopped practicing magic as therapy, or as a feel-good hobby, this is the guy that can show you what's real. He isn't an adviser. He isn't a tour guide. He is a pilot. He is the god that will make sure you don't miss anything. If you like seeing the world from the comfort of an air-conditioned tourist bus, Anubis is not for you. But if you are the human that says, "I want to see the real Egypt/Mexico/India – take me to the real market, the forbidden ruins, the site of the ceremonies the government claims don't happen anymore!" Then Anubis Airways is the best way to fly.

**Don Webb**

## BIBLIOGRAPHY FOR PART I & III

Bard, Kathryn A., Steven Blake Shubert, *Encyclopedia of the archaeology of ancient Egypt*, Routledge, 1999
Botterweck, G. Johannes, Helmer Ringgren, Heinz-Josef Fabry, *Theological dictionary of the Old Testament,* Volume 7, Wm. B. Eerdmans Publishing, 1995
Breasted, J.H., *Ancient Records of Egypt*, Vol I, The First through the Seventeenth Dynasties, 2001 (originally appeared in 1906)
Brier, Bob, *Ancient Egyptian Magic*, Quill, 1980
Brunton, Dr. Paul., *A Search in Secret Egypt* Samuel Weiser, Inc York Beach, Maine, 1988
Budge, E A Wallis., *The Book of Opening the Mouth*, Paul Kegan, Trench, Trubner, London 1909
Budge, E.A. Wallis., *The Gods of the Egyptians*, Vol. II, Dover, 1969
Davidson, Hilda Ellis., *The lost beliefs of northern Europe*, Routledge, 1993.
Denise M. Doxey., *The Ancient Gods Speak*, Redford, Donald B., Editor, Oxford University Press, 2002
Dodson, A., Hilton, D., *The Complete Royal Families of Ancient Egypt*, Thames & Hudson, 2004.
Faulkner, Raymond, O., *The Ancient Egyptian Pyramid Texts*, Oxford at the Clarendon Press, 1969
Faulkner, Raymond, O, *The Egyptian Book of the Dead*, Chronicle Books, 1998
Faulkner, Raymond, O., *A Concise Dictionary of Middle Egyptian*, Griffith Institute, 1999
Giddy, Lisa L, *The Anubieion at Saqqâra II. The Cemeteries*, Egypt Exploration Society Excavation Memoirs 56, London, 1992
Griffiths, J. Gwyn., *Plutarch's De Iside et Osiride*. University of Wales Press, ed. 1970.
Hagen, Rose-Marie and Rainer, *Egypt, People, Gods, Pharaohs*, Taschen, 1999
Hart, George, *Egyptian Myths*, British Museum Publications-University of Texas Press, 1990
*Herodotus, The Histories*, translated by R. Waterfield 1998, Oxford University Press: Oxford.
Hichens, Robert, *Spell of Egypt*, The Century Co New York 1911

Hobson, Christine, *The World of the Pharaohs*, Thames and Hudson, 1987

Hornung, Erik, *The Secret Lore of Egypt- Its Impact on the West*, Cornell University Press, 2002.

Ikram, S. and Dodson, A. *The Mummy in Ancient Egypt: Equipping the Dead for Eternity*, Thames and Hudson: London, 1998.

Ikram, S. *Death and Burial in Ancient Egypt*, Pearson: Edinburgh and London, 2003.

Issue 2, July-August 2000, *Cult and Funerary Temples*. Kemet Magazine

Issue 3, September-October 2000, *The Temple of Horus at Edfu*. Kemet Magazine

Issue 4, November-December 2000, *Myth and Ritual in the Temple of Horus at Edfu*. Kemet Magazine

Jeffreys, David G. and Smith, Harry S., *The Anubieion at Saqqâra I. The Settlement and the Temple Precinct*, Egypt Exploration Society Excavation Memoirs 54, London: 1988.

Kristensen, W. Brede trans., Hendricus Jacobus Franken, George R. H. Wright., *Life out of Death: Studies in the Religions of Egypt and of Ancient Greece* Leuven, BD: Peters Press, 1992

Logan, Thomas J. *The Origins of the Jmy-wt Fetish* Journal of the American Research Center in Egypt, 1990 Vol. 2

Lurker, Manfred., *Lexikon der Götter und Symbole der alten Ägypter*, Scherz 1998

Maspero, Gaston, *The Dawn of Civilization*, V. 1-A), ECA Associates, NY, 1991

Meeks, Dimitri and Meeks, Christine Favard, *Daily Life of the Egyptian Gods*, Cornell University Press, 1996

Morenz, Siegreied, *Egyptian Religion*, Cornell University Press, 1960

Naydler Jeremy, *Temple of the Cosmos Rochester, Vermont: Inner Traditions, 1996*

Page, Judith, *The Song of Set,* Æon Publishing, London, 2000

Page, Judith, *The Song of Meri Khem,* Mandrake of Oxford 2000

Page, Judith, *Pathworking with the Egyptian Gods*, Llewellyn Publications, U.S., Illustrated edition, 2007

Page, Judith, *Invoking the Egyptian Gods*, Llewellyn Publications, U.S.; Illustrated edition, 2012

Page, Judith, *The Song of Bast,* Æon Publishing, London 2015
Page, Judith and Webb, Don, *Set The Outsider,* Æon Publishing, London 2017
Pinch, Geraldine, *Handbook of Egyptian Mythology,* ABC-CLIO, 2002
Pinch, Geraldine, *Magic in Ancient Egypt,* University of Texas Press, 1994
Shaw, Ian and Nicholson Paul, *The British Museum Dictionary of Ancient Egypt,* British Museum Press 1995
Taylor J. H. (Editor) *Ancient Egyptian Book of the Dead: a journey through the afterlife.* British Museum Press: London, 2010
Temple, Robert K. G., *The Sirius Mystery,* Inner Traditions Bear and Company, 1992
Vernus, P.. *Le Mythe d'un mythe, La pretendue noyade d'Osiris,* 1991
Watterson, Barbara, *Gods of Ancient Egypt,* Sutton Publishing, 2000
Wilkinson, Richard H., *The Complete Gods and Goddesses of Ancient Egypt,* Thames and Hudson, 2003
Winlock, H.E., *The Eleventh Egyptian Dynasty,* JNES, 1943
Wallis Budge E.A., *The Book of the Dead.* New York: Gramercy Books, 1995
Wallis Budge E.A., *Osiris and the Egyptian Resurrection,* Vol. 1 New York: G.P. Putnam's Sons, 1911

**To Write to the Authors**

Judith Page
**Judith.page29@gmail**. com

Don Webb
**writebydonwebb@gmail.com**

Made in the USA
Columbia, SC
18 January 2024